The Myth of the Monstrous Male

THE MYTH OF THE MONSTROUS MALE

OF THE

MONSTROUS MALE

AND OTHER FEMINIST FABLES

JOHN GORDON

Playboy Press · New York

Manufactured in the United States of America.
First edition.

Playboy Press/A Division of PEI Books, Inc.

Library of Congress Cataloging in Publication Data

Gordon, John, 1945–
    The myth of the monstous male, and other
feminist fables.

    Bibliography: p.
    1. Feminism. I. Title.
HQ1154.G626   305.4'2   81–82459
ISBN 0–87223–758–3   AACR2

ACKNOWLEDGMENTS

The publisher and author gratefully acknowledge permission to reprint from the following in this book:

"Women and the Spoils of Success" by Anne Taylor Fleming. Copyright © 1981 by The New York Times Company. Reprinted by permission.

Against Our Will. Copyright © 1975 by Susan Brownmiller. Reprinted by permission of Simon & Schuster, a division of Gulf & Western Corporation.

"The Feminist Attack on Smut" by Irving Kristol. Reprinted by permission of *The New Republic.*

Woman's Proper Place: A History of Changing Ideals and Practices, 1870 to the Present. Copyright © 1978 by Sheila M. Rothman. By permission of Basic Books, Inc., Publishers, New York.

The Natural Superiority of Women, Rev. Ed. Copyright 1952, 1953, © 1968, 1974 by Ashley Montagu. By permission of Macmillan Publishing Co., Inc.

The New Chastity. Copyright © 1972 by Midge Decter. By permission of Coward, McCann & Geoghegan.

The First Sex. Copyright © 1971 by Elizabeth Gould Davis. By permission of G. P. Putnam's Sons.

"Erotic Film Festival to Counter *Deep Throat,*" as it appeared in the *Providence Journal Bulletin,* December 4, 1980. Reprinted by permission of United Press International.

"Opponents of Flourishing Sex Industry Hindered by Its Open Public Acceptance" by William Serrin. Copyright © 1981 by The New York Times Company. Reprinted by permission.

Going Too Far: The Personal Chronicle of a Feminist. Copyright © 1977 by Robin Morgan. Reprinted by permission of Random House, Inc.

The Feminization of American Culture. Copyright © 1977 by Ann Douglas. Reprinted by permission of Alfred A. Knopf, Inc.

Sex Without Love. Copyright © 1980 by Russell Venoy. By permission of Prometheus Books.

The Descent of Woman. Copyright © 1972 by Elaine Morgan. By permission of Stein and Day Publishers.

Female Sexual Slavery. Copyright © 1979 by Kathleen Barry. By permission of Prentice-Hall, Inc.

Ulysses. by James Joyce. Copyright 1914, 1918 by Margaret Caroline Anderson and renewed 1942, 1946 by Nora Joseph Joyce. By permission of Random House, Inc.

The Women's Room. Copyright © 1977 by Marilyn French. By permission of Simon and Schuster.

Him/Her/Self. Copyright © 1974 by Peter Gabriel Filene. By permission of Harcourt Brace Jovanovich, Inc.

Senator Joe McCarthy. Copyright © 1959 by Richard H. Rovere. By permission of Harcourt Brace Jovanovich, Inc.

Pornography: Men Possessing Women. Copyright © 1981 by Andrea Dworkin. By permission of Putnam's Publishing Group.

Contents

Introduction

MEMORANDUM
SUBJECT: Feminism and sex
FROM: The author
TO: To the nice woman who once charged into my office waving a copy of a beer advertisement in the student newspaper, featuring a balloon-breasted, semi-dressed model, and boomed: "GOD! This is DISGUSTING! What are we going to DO about it?"

To the former colleagues of mine at Hamilton College who, when a student entrepreneur and showman had the bright idea of hiring a local stripper to enliven the moribund student assemblies, did everything but have him publicly guillotined in the name of offended womankind, and who produced, for their *jihad,* the memorable warcry "Sex is not funny!"

To the same people, who succeeded in having such atrocious utterances as "Cressida is a whore" stricken from all mimeographed student exercises, to be replaced with such okay utterances as "Frank is a thief."

To the same people, who have, reportedly, since succeeded in introducing censorship into the college bookstore; and who annually sponsor a lecture-and-performance weekend, the main function of which is to inform their male students, on behalf of the female student body, that they belong by birth to a contingent of rapacious scum.

To the people described to me by a friend of mine from another campus—the ones who, when a bunch of rowdy male students quite tastelessly outfitted and displayed an inflatable female dummy in the college library, spoke of it in terms of cross-burnings and *Kristallnacht* desecrations, damn near got the boys expelled (this at a time when convicted plagiarists are regularly docked a letter grade and told not to do it again), and weren't satisfied until the culprits had publicly abased themselves and recanted.

To the literary critics, amateur and professional, who are step by step reducing the list of nonsuspect books to the works of John Stuart Mill and Doris Lessing, with occasional admissions from the carefully screened *oeuvre* of Margaret Fuller and Virginia Woolf.

To the people, most of them women, who years ago induced a Cambridge friend of mine to routinely start carrying a set of earplugs with him, for use whenever he found himself at a dinner table opposite one of them.

To all of these people, and the others like them, who more than once have asked me, and others like me, how I can feel as I do about their slanders and fatuities, their spite and buffoonery, and still call myself—of all the gall —a feminist.

Here's how.

We begin with the following assumptions:

Women are not better than men. Men are not better than women. With few and minor exceptions, they are created, though not identical, equal, and any selective legal restriction on the rights of either is unjustifiable, and ought to be removed from the statute books as soon as it is discovered.

Assuming the (at the moment) probable and highly regrettable failure of the Equal Rights Amendment to be ratified, men and women of good will should continue to work, state by state and issue by issue, for what the ERA was meant to accomplish: the elimination from our laws of the doctrine that either sex is entitled to certain special privileges or subject to certain special burdens.

Women who wish or have to work should be given exactly the same opportunities as men; men who wish or have to stay at home minding the house and children should be given exactly the same respect as women. Neither office is intrinsically superior to the other; neither office ever was.

Women and men who in their actions regularly operate from the assumption that a person's sex delimits the range of his or her competence or virtue are at best deluded and should be set straight or, if adamant, scorned. Men and women who operate from the assumption that anyone is entitled to develop her or his capacities to the maximum extent possible in an imperfect world are right, and should be supported.

Men who for their own ends play on women's traditional vulnerability and submissiveness are reprehensible. Women who for their own ends play on men's traditional gallantry and *complaisance* are reprehensible.

Men who tell you that all women on some level want to be raped are sexual bigots, analogous to the white racists who used to say that blacks enjoyed their degradation. Women who tell you that all men on some level are rapists are sexual bigots, analogous to the white racists who used to say that blacks are animals.

That there have so far been no supreme woman geniuses is a fact owing to the same lamentable set of as-

sumptions according to which there have been no supreme woman monsters either; what Virginia Woolf said
would have happened to Shakespeare's sister would have
happened to Hitler's sister, too.

Although at this point we cannot say to what extent the
biological differences between the sexes are likely to
result in different patterns of behavior when each is given
its free choice, we can say for certain that earlier efforts
to impose separate orders based on accepted biological
laws have been gross, repressive, wasteful of human resources, and stupid. Accordingly, anyone of good will
ought, for the foreseeable future, to forget distinctions
based on such perceptions and treat other people primar-
ily according to their perceived wishes, without the me-
diation of cultural gender myths.

All of the above are, as I understand it, what used to
be the essential articles of faith of what was once called
"women's liberation." They are what Betty Friedan,
Germaine Greer, Simone de Beauvoir (to an extent),
Gloria Steinem (for a time), Jane O'Reilly, Elizabeth
Janeway, and most other prominent feminists were usually getting at.

I have an occasional disagreement with some of those
writers (mainly with the latter-day Steinem), but not with
their central program, as it was generally perceived in the
early, heady days of the movement. Like virtually all the
men I know, I fervently wished (and still wish) women
well in their efforts to remove whatever political, economic, and social inequalities remain. Politically, I believe that we should simply accept once and for all the
simple premise that in the modern age the word "man,"
when used in the Declaration of Independence, Constitution, Bill of Rights, and common law, must clearly be
taken to mean "man and woman." Economically, I believe that everyone should be paid according to perform-

ance, regardless of sex or anything else. Socially . . . No one, happily, can prescribe social behavior; but for the record, let me add my voice to the general prayer that both macho men and Kewpie-doll women will stay out of style for a long, long time.

In short, the standard feminist platform is one to which I, in common with many and perhaps most of this country's males, subscribe. So why, in heaven's name, have I felt moved to write a book that, inasmuch as the great majority of its targets are feminists, is fairly certain to be taken by some as a disgruntled male's attack against feminism?

The answer is that, also in common with many of the males of this country, I am indeed a somewhat disgruntled male, and getting more so all the time. My disaffection began, I think, about ten years ago, the day a female acquaintance called me a male chauvinist because I was holding a door open for a very pregnant and package-encumbered woman. It took a quantum leap the day a woman named Marcia Womangold struck a blow against sexual oppression by shooting a bullet through the window of a Cambridge bookstore that I patronize. It was cemented by my exposure to the demagogic campaign of Women Against Pornography to equate male lust with all pornography, all pornography with the sadomasochistic subgenre, and the sadomasochistic subgenre with nazism. It was roused further by my reading of Marilyn French's *The Women's Room,* and after that of the various tracts, notably *Against Our Will,* of which *The Women's Room* is simply the fictional expression.

Eventually, I was led to face the conclusion that has in fact long been obvious—that whatever it may be in principle, for the last ten years or so feminism has in fact been quite possibly the most prolific single fountainhead of fashionably malignant and fraudulent drivel on the national scene. A movement that began as a genuinely liberating call for a radical enlargement of freedom, generosity, and sympathy has increasingly come to be represented by the sour, the mean, and the dumb.

There may be all kinds of reasons for this sad development, but I think I know what the main one is. I think the problem begins where a lot of other problems begin as well, with sex—specifically, with the long-standing and as yet far from resolved discrepancy in the expectations with which men and women approach it. It has long been the major area of dispute between feminist women and men like myself who, by virtue of their positions on virtually every other issue, wish to consider ourselves on their side. In recent years especially, it has demonstrably been at the root of those contentious issues—rape laws, pornography, prostitution, the relation of male and female homosexuals to the movement, the definition of what constitutes sexual harassment and the appropriate legal means for discouraging it—that have increasingly come to occupy center stage and to separate the movement from many of its would-be supporters.

That, anyway, is the conclusion I come to when I read the newspapers, read through the canonical literature, or review my own baffled efforts, over the last several years, to reach some accommodation with feminism: You can be for the ERA and equal pay, for every imaginable legal, political, and social adjustment conducive to making women in every way equal to men, but it will avail you nothing if you once reveal yourself to be stimulated to anything but admiration by any of the well-known heterosexual cues, or tolerant of others so stimulated. "Aha," the feminists will say, "the sheep's clothing falls away at last, and the beast stands revealed in his lair." You will be accused of wanting to "exploit" (the word, for all intents and purposes, means "screw") women, of thinking "sexist" (meaning "sexual") and "chauvinist" (meaning "sexual") thoughts.

This fixation, so prominent lately, has had its origins in the movement's theorists and popularizers. By my own estimate, in the last twenty years the four feminist books that have had the widest impact have been *The Feminine Mystique, Sexual Politics, Against Our Will,* and *The Women's Room.* Of those four, three operate from the assumption that women's woes are traceable to the nature of the male libido: *Sexual Politics* is about heterosexual pornography, and how it is paradigmatic of the relation between men and women; *Against Our Will* is about rape, and how it is paradigmatic of the relation between men and women; *The Women's Room* opens with an attempted rape and concludes with a successful one, and features a cast of men who typically dabble in writing sadistic pornography and sound like this:

"Hey, come here, Mommy, Baby wanna suck your boobs. Little Billy cold, Mommy, need little Blissy come play with him."

So this book is about feminism and sex. About feminism and money, feminism and politics, feminism and anything else, it has nothing particular to say, except insofar as they intersect the central subject. Except for that one subject, my feeling is that it's all pretty much been said many times already by feminists themselves, and that I agree. Women have faced all those other issues squarely, and come up with reasonable, commendable positions. What they haven't faced is the potentially ruinous contradiction between those positions and the implications of their continuing, and at the moment escalating, campaign against male lust. Yet that, clearly, is the issue of the hour, on which the success of the whole agenda may well turn. It's time we faced that one, too.

1

Past and Present

T HE GUYS I really feel sorry for," said my friend Neil to me one night, "are the ones ten to twenty years younger than us."

"Us," I should explain, is the baby-boom generation, the ones whose collective youth helped make the Sixties so energetic and whose accumulating middle age has helped make the present so enervating. I am thirty-six; Neil is thirty-seven.

"You look at a demographic chart," said Neil, "and the people our age look like a pet lamb going through a python. I mean, we're *it*. We call the tune, and we're going to keep calling it for the next thirty years, until we start dropping off in serious numbers. Even then, the top forty will start being full of folky ballads about dying with dignity.

"It used to piss off our parents like crazy, this lock we had on the *Zeitgeist*. Remember the generation gap? But it must be even worse for the ones behind us, the kids today. Imagine it: always being secondhand, always being out of it. Being made to feel puerile into your fifties, probably. Have you seen the ones trying to live up

3

to the way we were at their age? Pathetic. We had the
Beatles and Dylan . . . What have they got? Punk and
junk. And the ones trying to imitate the way we are now
are even worse. All those teddibly soigné Alligator jokes.
You show me a kid making Alligator jokes, I'll show you
a twenty-year-old pretending he's forty.

"But the worst part must be the sex. The great thing
about sex for us was the timing. We hit puberty in the late
Fifties, when the party line on sex was still pretty brutal,
and girls would spend long hours laying it down to one
another about whether they should let a guy kiss them on
the first date and all that. What I mean to say is that most
of us had to go through a hell of a lot to get a little. For
at least a few years, almost every one of us was programmed into being a fiend on the subject. If my fairy
godmother had given me my wish when I was sixteen,
there's no doubt at all what it would have been: 'Fairy
godmother,' I'd have said, 'I want to get laid whenever
I want.'

"And then, around about 1964—gangbusters. I'm
rubbing my eyes and I can't believe it. I'm in college
then, and the girls are something else—I mean literally
something else, like caterpillar and butterfly. They are
protesting parietal hours—in some places they are getting parietal hours abolished. Suddenly they are all carrying around those birth-control-pill cases, which are
cleverly disguised as compacts for when their mothers go
through their purses.

"The president of a women's college where I spend a
weekend or two gives a speech telling them that, if they
don't shape up, everyone will think they're tramps and
tarts, and they laugh at him. It becomes known as the
tramp-and-tart speech, and they're making jokes about it,
and he's suddenly everyone's idea of an asshole, and he
can't show his face on campus again.

"My old tormentor, Mrs. Weatherwax, the

housemother who all through my freshman year kept telling me I couldn't step across the line that divides the reception room of my girlfriend's dormitory from the sleeping area—if I had a nickel for every time she told me, 'You've got to draw the line somewhere,' I'd have a lot of nickels—gets sent packing in tears to draw her lines somewhere else.

"Later, a different girlfriend calls up my roommate and tells him that *her* roommate feels burdened by her virginity—that's how she put it—and would he please come over sometime soon and give her a friendly fuck. Which he does, while my girlfriend and I go out to get a bottle of champagne, which we all drink together afterward—'After the fall,' my girlfriend's roommate puts it. A few years earlier, if I'd even dreamed of something like that, it would have meant that my fantasies were getting dangerously out of control.

"And so on, until there comes a night in the summer of 1969—it's about the time of the moon landing—when I find myself in New York one late afternoon, needing a place to spend the night, and I realize that there are eleven different women I can call up with a reasonably good chance of getting taken in, provided they're not already engaged. And I say to myself, Neil, this is it. Stop the clock right now, because this is the way it should be and it is never going to be any better.

"Well, you know the story after that. Vitamin E. Dieting. Jogging. The *Wall Street Journal.* I become the bloated and balding facsimile of my former self which you now see before you, happily married and doing well —wouldn't have it any other way—but also sustained by the memory of the time when we had it all.

"It wasn't just being young and all that. It was passing from Fifties sex to Sixties sex—as if some sweetheart of a god made it a point to give you a few years to stoke up your fantasies, getting you primed to scrabble and haggle

5

and wheedle and do just about anything necessary, and then suddenly said, 'Hey, relax, what's with all the sweat? You want lots of sex, you can have lots of sex.'

"Have you ever known a Jack Mormon? That's a life-long Mormon who suddenly drops out of the church and starts trying out all the things at once that have been off limits. I knew one once, and I mean to say I never saw anyone who knew how to have such a good time. That's what we were, coming from the Fifties into the Sixties— Jack Mormons. We did our hitch in the wilderness, and then all at once there was the Jordan, cool and sweet and flowing on, it seemed, forever. First the desert, then the oasis—just the way it's supposed to be. That's what I mean when I say that our timing was perfect.

"But these kids—their timing is *lousy.* They are set up to get the absolute worst of both worlds. They were born in the oasis, and grew up thinking it was just the natural order of things; meanwhile, the desert keeps getting closer. Do you know what one of them said to me the other day? He told me that sex wasn't everything. Nineteen years old, telling me that sex isn't everything. He told me that sex without love was empty, and that only when two people really loved one another in a spiritual way was it a truly meaningful experience. I am not making this up. I believe he even used the words 'mere sex.' Mere sex! Have you ever noticed how useful that word 'mere' is? Mere pleasure. Mere happiness. Mere sunshine. Mere good. Mere sex, for Christ's sake!

"I will say this for the kid. I have met his girlfriend, who has a face and figure and way about her that would rouse the blood of a dried cod, and I am reasonably certain that he is experiencing some pretty fine mere sex and that what he, I swear to you, called the 'spirituality aspect' is not quite as *sine qua non* as he would have me believe. In fact, I will say in his behalf that I believe he was lying, and that he probably knew it.

6

"The fact remains that he felt called upon to come out with that crock of shit, and he probably has to come out with it fairly regularly for her, too, if he doesn't want to get shut out. And do you know why? Because he and his girlfriend are a couple of those poor shmucks stuck in the backwash of our generation, which means that for most of their lives they're going to be parroting secondhand copies of things people our age are saying. Thanks to us, the national hormonal level is dropping like southern California water tables, and he and his pals are caught up in the general drag.

"For most of us—not for you and me, of course, old buddy, but still, for most of the people our age—sex is getting more mere with every year. So the idea starts circulating that, on second thought, maybe it's not so hot after all, compared to, say, tax-free municipal bonds. The really pathetic thing is that some of these kids are buying it. I mean, here's a guy, nineteen years old and healthy, probably has to do transcendental meditation or something every morning to get rid of his hard-on so he can go out and face the world, going on about mere sex. It just goes to show. It makes you able to understand those poor bastards in Jonestown more. Some people can be brainwashed into anything.

"So it looks like what's going to happen is that they're going to have to learn the awful facts of life all over again. Like the man said, those who don't learn from history are condemned to run through the sucker again until they finally get it right. They want all that shit back, let them see how they like it. Let them have their Fifties revival.

"Jesus, the Fifties. Only people who weren't around during the Fifties could even think of such a thing. Us, we remember what the Fifties were. Remember that automobile ad from around 1957 that went, 'Suddenly, it's 1960'? That was a very astute advertisement, because even then everybody knew that the sooner the Fifties were over, the better. You and me, we're about as likely to join in a Fifties revival as old Wermacht veterans are to take nostalgic sentimental journeys back to Stalingrad.

"For me, for instance, a Fifties revival would mean rubbing my face all over with bacon grease for days until it resembled the moon; then taking some girl dressed in what looks like a helium balloon to a restaurant, where she'd talk about *The Good Earth* and try to smoke cigarettes; then to a dance, where we'd scrunch against one another to Johnny Mathis records until I'm about doubled over with gonadal congestion; then to a car, where I would finally find out, as they used to put it, whether I'd played my cards right. If you haven't, you're a shmendrik, and everyone knows about it within forty-eight hours; and if you have, then that means, lucky you, you've won her heart, and if you don't call her up the next morning and propose marriage, she starts looking at you with the kind of look a calf gets just before it gets knocked on the head.

"That's what the Fifties means. That's what it was like before almost all of us, almost all at once, saw through that 'mere sex' bullshit. Now some of them want it to come back. Poor wienies. They just have no idea how really awful it all was. It's depressing, but I'm happily out of it now, and it's their lookout. Now if you'll excuse me, I have to get some mere sleep."

Whatever was Neil talking about? Not really about the present population of young Americans, if the statistics about their level of sexual activity are to be believed. Rather, he was predicting the future, operating from the tried and tested theory that what certain influential people are saying today will be the common currency in a few years' time. No doubt he was thinking of the latest

risorgimento of the American right, but not so much
about the right by itself as about the way its plans for our
private lives, these days, seem to dovetail strangely with
what has become of the most enduring liberation movement inherited from the Sixties, feminism.

In fact, he was mainly talking about feminism, and how
it has changed since appearing on the national scene
around 1969. Insofar as the feminist movement can be
said to reflect American women's collective ideas of what
their interests are and how to achieve them, its current
state does indeed seem to be an index of some wide-
spread female return to Fifties fables, and behind those
fables the traditional object-to-subject relationship of
woman to man. Noting in *The New Republic* the evidence
of such a return while reviewing one of several recent
feminist books urging that pornography is part of a masculine conspiracy to degrade women and ought to be
squelched, New Right essayist Irving Kristol is gratified
to observe:

It was utterly predictable that freedom of pornographic speech
and action would sooner or later come into conflict with the
women's movement. Pornography, after all, has long been
recognized to be a predominantly male fantasy involving the
sadistic humiliation of women. The women's movement itself,
however, did not foresee any such conflict. On the contrary:
it assumed a perfectly natural congruence between "sexual
liberation" and "women's liberation." Indeed, it was this assumption that differentiated what in the 1960s we came to call
"women's lib" from the traditional "feminist" movement that
is now at least a century and a half old. Whereas feminists
demanded more equal treatment and respect for women, corresponding to the more equal status they were in fact achieving
in modern society, the movement for women's liberation pro-
posed to create a radically new human condition for both men
and women. There was relatively little utopianism in the feminist movement, which was essentially meliorist and adaptive.

Women's liberation, in contrast, was utopian in essence, and it was only because it managed to co-opt the feminist impulse that so many were confused as to its ultimate intentions. Today, the unravelling of the movements is well under way. Feminism survives as a sturdy and successful enterprise; women's liberation is enmeshed in intellectual and practical dilemmas.

Aside from his bland equation of pornography with humiliation, which is nonsense, Kristol has observed the current state of affairs accurately enough. Feminism—women's liberation is indeed unraveling, as more of its leading members return to the "purity crusade" rhetoric that was once synonymous with the woman's cause, and abandon the ideas of sexual freedom with which their movement for the most part began, thirteen or so years ago.

This book's main thesis is that such a return, if continued, is certain to prove fatal to any coherent feminist vision of sexual equality now in currency. I think that such a return must of necessity reinstate and reinforce the double standard, and that the double standard is incompatible with the equal sharing of rights and responsibilities between men and women.

But there is another, more personal reason for being upset about the prospect of such a return. It is my memory, which I share with Neil and which he recalled to me, of how awful it once was.

I was reminded of that myself, a little while ago, while on a train crowded with college students going home for spring vacation. Since there weren't any free seats to move to, I had no way of escaping the loud conversation of the young woman, perhaps eighteen years old, holding forth in the aisle just behind me. This was about how it went:

"You know, I don't really like to drink all that much, but I *really* like these seven-and-sevens."

Then some tediously detailed narrative about the boring lives of her peers. Then:

"Boy, I have to tell you, these seven-and-sevens are really terrific. I mean, you know, I'm not a big drinker or anything, but I *really, really* like these seven-and-sevens."

Followed by more boring stories, along with some political analysis ("That Ayatollah is a real asshole, you know?"), and then, so help me:

"I could drink these seven-and-sevens all day long. I'm not really into drinking or anything, but I really do go for seven-and-sevens."

And later—yes, after delivering herself of the observation that the prospect of being away from school for two weeks was a pleasant one:

"Man, I'm going to go get myself another seven-and-seven. I think they're terrific. And you know, the thing about me is, I'm usually not all that big a drinker. I don't drink much at all. But seven-and-sevens—I don't know, there's something about them. I really, really do go for these seven-and-sevens."

I was reminded of two things. First, I was reminded of certain feminist theorists who say that the conversation of females, because less specialized and goal-oriented than the conversation of males, is more in tune with the true and the beautiful. They are obviously out of their minds.

Second, I was reminded of similar or identical conversations in the late Fifties and early Sixties, back in that slough of despond whose remembrance Neil and I have in common.

"Seven-and-sevens": It was, to conflate a couple of literary allusions, like a *madeleine* bringing back the world of the blacking factory. How many young women, in those days, had informed me of their enthusiasm for seven-and-sevens again and again—endured, indulged, sheltered from the news, which would have been freely dispensed to any male, of how boring they were being?

I remembered the phalanxes of females leaving the table to march in formation to the ladies' room, there to hammer out a platform on each one's date. I remembered that, as often as not, they called the ladies' room the "little girl's room." I remembered those who drank beer being frequently incapable of running off to it without informing us that the thing about beer was that it went right through them.

I remembered the letters—written in fuchsia ink, *i*'s dotted with little smile faces, full of exclamation marks!, signed with a single discreet initial, stamp reversed.

I remembered the intense conversations. Kahlil Gibran. The symbolism of *The Seventh Seal.* Her religious philosophy: "I don't believe in a god, exactly; I believe in a sort of universal good."

I remembered the indescribable feculence of the taste of tobacco smoke licked out from the inside of someone else's mouth. The humid passion pits. The repartee: "Are you Italian? You've sure got roamin' hands." The escalating progression of prizes along that monkish map of Middle Earth, her body, each to be won, like a giant's horde in a Grimm's tale, by a new incantation at each stage, delivered with the right mix of hardiness and guile.

The silliness; the enforced abjectness; the multiple variations of mandated bad faith; the popular gambit, outlined in the time's most symptomatic best seller, *Games People Play,* called "Let's You and Him Fight" ("Are you going to let him get away with that?"); the euphemisms for "He has money" or "Does he have money?"; the code words for "marriage" or "relationship likely to lead to marriage with all deliberate speed"; the battery of feints, cues, and gestures the effective gist of which always turned out to be the same: *"Lie to me; lie to me; lie to me."* The all but universal female code expressed in that folk-wisdom proverb, "If he can get all the milk he wants, why should he buy a cow?"; the all but universal female neurosis expressed in a popular song of the period:

Every girl wants someone who
She can always look up to.
You know I love you, of course.
Let me know that you're the boss!

[CHORUS]   Johnny get angry, Johnny get mad,
Give me the biggest lecture I ever had.
I want a brave man, I want a cave man,
Johnny show me that you care, really care for me.

Lord. As Neil would put it: All that bullshit, just to get laid.

So put this in the time capsule: Never believe any female polemist who tells you that the grief in those days was all being dished out by men to women. And never let it be said, unchallenged, that the old ways were best, that they produced ladies and gentlemen, for instance— civilized creatures trained through customs of mutual restraint to bring their urges into a harmony, like the harmony between artifice and nature in a formal garden.

What they produced, in that there garden, was bonsai and brambles: women pretending to be porcelain paragons for reasons of the most obvious and squalid self-interest; and men, for similar reasons, reinforcing them in their fatuities—a play between meretriciousness and exacerbated lust, with all the attendant ugliness, greed, and cruelty. Neil was right: It was awful, for Johnny as well as for his girlfriend.

Here, with names and some details of course altered, are four illustrative recollections from the era:

1. *Time: 1955–56.*   A meeting of a Boy Scout troop.

The scoutmaster announces that one of the boys was caught stealing at a recent public function at which members of the troop had been ushers. The boy has a choice of atonements: He can turn himself in to the police, or he can run the gauntlet.

He chooses to run the gauntlet. This means that he takes off his shirt and undershirt and runs between two lines of Scouts, about forty or fifty in number, each of whom is instructed to take a cut at him with the canvas length and brass clasp of his Boy Scout belt. Then he runs back the other way, with the action repeated.

The experience makes an impression on me—not to mention the impression it makes on its main actor. To this day, it is what I automatically think of when I encounter either of two words—"macho" and "welt." The quivering, chicken-white form of the boy stumbling into the outspread arms of the scoutmaster at the end of his return trip, as if being welcomed into some obscure mystery that awaits everyone in the room, is something that, I record with gratitude, feminism taught me finally to understand, and hate.

2. *Time: About 1963.* This one is quite possibly only a legend. It is the kind of story commonly told about men in rival colleges or fraternities—just as, according to anthropologists, it is always the next tribe upriver that practices cannibalism. Anyway, it was told at my college about the men at another college, and, true or not, it strikes me as emblematic.

The story is about a fraternity whose members once every year hold what they call a "pig party"—the idea of the party being that everyone bring the ugliest girl he knows; that the invited guests not be told the principle of selection but be allowed to figure it out for themselves while the members are getting drunk and passing out; and that at some point in the evening a vote be taken and a trophy be awarded to the least attractive date present.

In the version I heard, the tradition comes to an end when one of the members shows up with a girl in a wheelchair, thus—as we used to put it—grossing out even his brothers.

3. *Time: 1963.* This one is definitely not a legend— the people were real. One was a sweet, somewhat retiring premed; the other was his former high-school girl-friend and, through seven and a half college semesters, fiancée.

They were, everyone knew, inseparable. They had decided on when they were going to get married, where they would live, how many children they would have. Their engagement, as it turned out, lasted just one week longer than the boy's medical career, one week past the night he told her, while reportedly in something like despair, that the last of the medical schools to which he had applied had just rejected him, and that he wasn't going to be a doctor after all.

The girl called up her mother. They had a long talk, and agreed at the end that he was indeed a very nice boy but that the engagement had been made under what it now seemed clear were false pretenses—they'd both thought he was a better student than *that;* and that, although as a senior the girl had wasted almost her whole college career, still many fine young men were getting married fairly late these days and, being pretty and having, as everyone always said, "personality plus," in addition to a good reputation (not surprisingly, since she had been out of circulation for about six years), she could still hope to land a winner if she didn't waste any more time.

Report has it that she is now married to a general practitioner in the greater Baltimore area, where she perhaps passes her days wondering whether her life would have been happier with the sweet loser she crushed so efficaciously, or, on the other hand, perhaps wonders whether, if she'd ditched him sooner, she might have netted a specialist.

4. *Time: 1964.* The word for Veronica was "superb." She was tall, sinewy, electric, unassimilated. One of her many enthusiasms, which she was more inclined to celebrate than to conceal, was for sex. She thought it was great. It never occurred to her, as far as I can recall, to mete it out in return for other things. When she realized, one day, that the day before she had slept with three different men—having waked up with one, gone to bed with another, and met an old friend in between—her reaction was to whoop loudly and write a story about it (she was a splendid writer).

Some people—some women, to be frank about it— were anxious to tell you that she must be insecure and ought to be pitied, but the fact was that no one around her seemed to be having half so good a time.

The girls in her dormitory simply hated her. They made this clear in a number of ways—often, for reasons I leave to others, by attacking her clothes. One of them simply threw her clothes out of her second-story window; Veronica came back from class to find them hanging from the tree opposite her window and strewn across the ground beneath. Someone, more resourceful, stole her wet laundry out of the washing machine, wrapped it into a bundle, and stashed it in the dormitory kitchen's freezer, thus reducing it to one big heavy icy ball. Someone else sneaked into her room while she was in the shower and scissored the crotches out of her panties—an innuendo no doubt picked up from the Frederick's of Hollywood catalog. Infinite changes were rung on the fact that her initials were V.D. Graffiti employing this and similar conceits appeared on walls throughout the dormitory. Parties were announced to which everyone was invited but her. Finally, at the end of the year, she escaped to Bennington—which God knows had problems of its own, but which was at least free of this brand of prematurely matronly esprit de corps.

At the time, hearing of these things second- and third hand, I could only conclude that something dreadful automatically comes over women when isolated in herds. In my copy of *Vanity Fair,* which I was reading for class at the time, I happened across and underlined the following passage, writing Veronica's real name next to it:

"I must tell you again we're not in a barrack, William," Ann remarked.

"In a barrack, by Jove—I wish anybody in a barrack would say what you do," cried out this uproused British lion. "I should like to hear a man breathe a word against her, by Jupiter. But men don't talk in this way, Ann: it's only women, who get together and hiss, and shriek, and cackle."

Experience and reflection have, since then, modified my opinion. The girls around Veronica were not illustrating what happens when the female of the species reverts to type. Rather, they were illustrating what happens when a bunch of mean-minded little squits of whatever sex, raised to artificially inflate its value by pretty much cornering the local market on what another group wants, is confronted by someone manifestly superior who, furthermore, threatens a breach in the cartel. The behavior was not particularly female—the Teamsters have been known to behave similarly under similar marketplace pressures. It was merely mean, common, and low—the way some human beings, especially those accustomed to thinking of themselves as commodities, tend to act under certain circumstances.

Twelve years after the end of the Sixties and at the beginning of feminism's second wave, that stands out for me as the moral of these four little-remembered horror stories. The old order had a way of bringing out a certain

kind of nastiness—whether of men to men (story number
1), men to women (story number 2), women to men
(story number 3), or women to women (story number
4). It was not, as some feminist memorialists would have
you believe, a period simply of men abusing women;
women were at least as accomplished at such things. For
both sexes, it was a time of the most outlandish and
degrading contortions, justified, ironically enough, with
appeals to nature: That was just the way men were (numbers 1 and 2); that was just the way women were (numbers 3 and 4).

It would please me to think that the reader might keep
those four cautionary tales in mind during the coming
dumb years, as the Moral Majority establishes itself in
Washington and from there metastasizes its wretched
way toward our private lives, because for sure we're in
for a heavy dose of such "nature" homilies again, along
with appeals for a return to the pre-Pill days of chivalric
men and maidenly maids.

The groundwork has already been laid, for instance by
Christopher Lasch, whose best seller, *The Culture of Narcissism,* has no patience at all with the "pseudoliberated
woman" of today; and by George Gilder, favorite social
theorist of the Reaganites, who argues that the traditional
female prerogative of sexual blackmail has always been
the main thing preventing civilization's collapse into savagery, and that women had better get back to it pretty
soon.

We can expect more of that sort of talk, stretched out
with metaphors drawn from horticulture and natural history, punched up with statistics on teen-age pregnancy
and warnings about herpes simplex, prettified with Cart-
landian furbelows. The thing to keep in mind is just what
Neil reminded me of: that it is all, without exception,
bullshit. Whatever the strains in the present uneasy truce
between the sexes, what we are going to be asked to

reinstate was much worse. What we will be asked to return to, underneath the nostalgia and the middle-aged recantations, equals pig parties and the marriage Mafia of mom and daughter—pigs and prigs. Only this time everyone will, underneath it all, know that it's a fraud.

As Neil points out, the generation he and I have in common has the distinction of having proclaimed the fraud for what it was. Or, to give credit where due, the women did. For the most part, the sexual revolution was brought about by a change not in male attitudes toward sex—which have in fact been admirably consistent for a long time—but in female attitudes: Women simply stopped pretending to believe in all that nonsense. Looking back, that—aside from the other generally adduced causes (the Pill, penicillin, the waning of religious and familial influence)—is what stands out as the major cause: Women simply got tired of pretending. They were weary of being saddled with maintaining fictions that any idiot could see through.

That, anyway, is my recollection. By the opening years of the Sixties, the level of skepticism about the old sexual dispensation had for some time been at or near the level that has continued to this day. Perhaps there had been a time—proverbially ascribed to the Age of Chivalry, which everyone agreed was dead—when women who saved themselves (meaning their pubic region) for one man could honestly feel ennobled in some vaguely religious way. But that time was past. For years men had been doing their best to laugh it to extinction; and when the women started laughing, too, the jig was up. Because without the sustaining mythology, the traditional female tactics for resistance were reduced to one of two things: a species of backwardness, or a species of mendacity. A certain amount of what was known as seduction consisted of pointing out that fact. (A certain amount of the rest consisted of liquor.)

Thus the sexual revolution, as many people have pointed out, was not so much a conversion—in fact the numbers didn't change all that much—as an open acknowledgment: Everyone suddenly agreed that there was just no good reason anymore for women not to enjoy themselves, sexually or otherwise.

And with that acknowledgment, feminism became possible once again. There were, of course, other powerful influences at work. Feminist historians have stressed—probably overstressed—the example of the civil-rights movement to women, who began to draw analogies between themselves and the emerging blacks; and in general a wide range of historical forces, forces beyond the conscious choice of any individual, needed to come to culmination before the idea of genuine sexual equality could become imaginable. But there was one choice that was in the control of individual women: They could continue to think of their bodies, and the selves within them, as icons, or they could choose to think of them as agents. Many women chose the latter, and the decision was crucial. It was indispensable for the rise of feminism, in two major ways.

First, it was itself a precondition for liberation—an affirmation of independence, freedom, and selfhood. I can now see how demeaning it must have been for females my age—raised in the same century, capable of the same mental processes—to be given the role of defending something the hollowness of which they could fail to recognize only by the blankest know-nothingism, the ethos of which they could defend only with the crassest mercantilism. "I felt," a woman was to describe it later, "like one of those madonnas with dollar bills pinned to her robe that are carried around at Italian festivals"—and, yes, that was the seamy little game, as it lay exposed in the early Sixties: rather than the traditional polarity between madonna and whore, a gradation of prices, of bids, linking one to the other, the bids determined by the woman's overall physical plant, combined with her mastery of the crudest principles of supply and demand.

A typical joke of the period:

MAN: Would you sleep with a stranger for a million dollars?
WOMAN: Yes, to be honest, I probably would.
MAN: Will you sleep with me for a dollar?
WOMAN: Certainly not! What do you take me for?
MAN: We've established what you are, madam; now we're just haggling over the price.

The collective decision by many young women of the time to take the price tags off themselves was an essential first step for their demand, which was to follow shortly, to be treated as full-fledged human beings. Before, they had made themselves, with their skittishness, coyness, makeup, "reputation" grapevine, and, when necessary, the cutting of the crotches out of some renegade's panties, into bodies to be coveted and haggled over. That is, they had made themselves into what we were later to call "objects." Now they were going to be subjects, too. In the process, they were putting behind them a good deal of what it had traditionally meant to be "feminine." It was only a matter of time—only a few years, in fact—before they started thinking of jettisoning the rest.

For decades the idea had been around that women were entitled to equal opportunity and equal pay—the ERA had long been a plank in the Republican party platform, an occasional woman would occupy a nonvital Cabinet post, and the "doctor" who turned out to be Raquel Welch or some such was a staple of Hollywood adventures—but it was one of those ideas that everyone acknowledges and no one takes seriously. There was too much evidence that women, for the most part, didn't want it to be taken seriously. A creature who insists on her specialness, her delicacy, and precious apartness is not a creature likely to feel at home in medical school or the union hall, and the sexual contract as it existed at the time required that women hold themselves aloof and adopt the poses of aloofness.

It was only after they had at least partially rejected those poses that women—and men—could rediscover that vision of genuine sexual equality which had lain dormant in the national consciousness since women got the vote. It was only by dropping their traditional passive resistance in the battle between the sexes that women could become active in other ways as well.

That was one major way in which feminism was an outgrowth of the sexual revolution. There was a second, which was and is fundamentally at odds with the first— so much so, in fact, that few feminist advocates have been willing to face, let alone resolve, the contradiction, and "feminism" at this late date continues to be a repertoire of often mismatched poses rather than a coherent set of principles. Put simply, the women who were trying to bridge the discrepancies between the sexes by adopting the traditional license of men found themselves countered by a growing number of women who wished instead to resolve the gap by hectoring and legislating men up to their own traditionally exalted level. It was the old Robespierre lesson all over again: a liberation movement turning repressive, almost overnight. It was the beginning of feminism's lamentable evolution into what today strikes many people as simply a trendy species of intolerance, and the source of what today stands as the most ominous danger to the movement's future.

Since at least Kate Millett's shocked discovery, in *Sexual Politics,* that some pornography really was just as brutal as the older generation said it was, the movement has often seemed to be mainly one of revulsion against what women had found out about men and their world during the years 1964–70, when all us men had assumed they were having the time of their lives. It turned out that we had been wrong about that. They intended to see to it that we didn't make that mistake again.

If in one way women's liberation had clearly evolved from the new morality, in another way it was, just as clearly, a backlash against it. It was not just in the imagination of a few scarified male chauvinists that feminists seemed to be man-haters. The literature of the movement was, and is, shot through with testimony to the fact, and the single clearest point to emerge when you talked to its members was that being in favor of equal pay for equal work and the rest of the package was not enough; what was required was nothing short of a fundamental change in the male attitude toward women—which was to say, in male sexuality.

That, somehow, was what it always seemed to come down to: sex. Stop treating us like pieces of meat. Don't look at us that way. "This exploits women"—a sticker invariably attached to some ad featuring a cheesecake picture. The word "exploitation" itself became, three or four years after the movement got started, *the* factotum of feminist rhetoric. Difficult to define, its meaning, as far as I was ever able to make out, slides between the very general "anything bad done by men to women" and the very specific "sex without adequate compensation"— compensation usually turning out to be some trendy variant of marriage.

In other words, "exploit" was just the latest version of "screw," its virulence deriving from its unstable blending of the literal and the figurative. Women were complaining about the conditions of their participation in the sexual act—which meant, in effect, that they were demanding something in return. Which, as it happened, had been exactly what they used to demand. For a certain influential number of women, the old code had changed its terminology but stayed substantially the same.

I can see two possible ways of accounting for this back-lash element in feminism. The first is just to say, re-signedly, that sexual differentiation, and the differing attitudes that result from it, is fundamental, immutable, bound to resist, in the long run, any utopian plans for human perfectibility: *Plus ça change, plus c'est la même chose.*

The argument goes like this: Despite the Pill and the rest of the contraceptive arsenal, a woman making love with a man still knows somewhere in her cells that if by chance anyone here gets pregnant, it ain't going to be him.

Also, however nice he may be, however safe she may feel with him, there's still the fact—woman's gym, Kung Fu, and Kama Sutra notwithstanding—that he almost cer-tainly outweighs her, could almost certainly outmuscle her, and is probably on top of her to boot. As one woman friend put it: "If *you* had someone outweighing you by fifty percent or so bouncing around on top of your body, *you'd* probably want him to tell you he loved you pretty often, too, don't you think?"

And then there's the act itself, which no matter how you slice it comes down to the penetration (they used to say violation) of her body, not his—an act that in any form has been surrounded in all cultures in all times with reverence and dread. There's also the universal associa-tion of that act with violence, often with violent death—and along with that, in the background, the fact of rape, an almost exclusively male crime committed mostly against women.

Then there are the other physiological differences: the uncertainty of his ability to perform, resulting in perhaps excessive urgency; the uncertainty of her ability to re-spond, resulting in perhaps excessive tentativeness; the well-documented disparity between their curves of arousal and subsidence.

How silly it can seem, facing this stratum of rock-bottom facts, that anyone could ever have imagined they could be ignored or legislated away. And the same goes for the logical consequences of these facts: that when it comes to sex, women have more at stake than men; that therefore it is and always will be, in the main, something that men try to get from women, and that women choose to selectively withhold from men. Which is to say that although women may intermittently resent their status as objects and protest it verbally, they will always in their actions elect it and work to reinforce it.

Viewed from this perspective, the recent progress of feminism, its steady shrinkage from the early blithe lubricity of Germaine Greer down to its current morbid, numbing fixation on pornography, prostitution, and all other forms of "exploitation," was simply inevitable. The logic behind the course of events is obvious: Men don't change; women don't change. It is simply woman's nature to keep the lid on sex. In the past, various substantial concerns have supported her in this role—the importance of her reputation, the fear of pregnancy, religious scruples, the supreme need to land one man. Then, in one five- to ten-year period, a crisis: All the old props seemed to have collapsed all at once. With no intellectually respectable basis for the old role, she floundered around for a few years, trying out some traditional male tomcattery and being, predictably, traumatized in the process. Something obviously needed to be done. If the old set of beliefs no longer served to justify her instincts, a new justification, drawing on other fields of discourse, had to be found or fashioned.

At the time (this was the Sixties, remember), the obvious field of the sort required was an uncoordinated, vaguely leftish ideology. Talk of "exploitation" was everywhere: It was what the white corporate state was doing to Vietnam, what it had done and was doing to blacks. Replace the word "white" with "male," shift the center of attention from the rice paddy and ghetto to the bedroom, make a few fine tunings, and you have, as has become increasingly obvious over the years, what feminism really boils down to: an ideological rationale for the immemorial application of female brakes to male libido, the old feminine crusade against sex, masquerading as a feminist campaign against sexism (nothing more revealing than the indiscriminate spatchcocking of those Sixties "ists" and "isms")—in short, Mrs. Grundy, in modern dress, at the barricades.

The first and best observer to point out the reactionary nature of what was then called "women's liberation" was Midge Decter, who in her 1972 book *The New Chastity* remorselessly demonstrated, with a logic and marshaling of evidence that feminists ever since have indignantly repudiated without bothering to refute, that in most ways that mattered the feminist program, insofar as it was detectable, amounted to a flight from freedom. (Or, as most of the movement's writers would put it, "freedom.") Ten years later, her observations are worth recalling at some length.

On work:

The movement says that women are being excluded from the centers of power in this society. Whereas the truth is that they —or at least those among them who agree to be spoken for by the movement—cannot tolerate the terms imposed on them by so much of power as they already enjoy. They have discovered that life for the venturesome provides, with each of its opportunities, a set of pitfalls, and they tend, quite naturally, to be frightened. "We don't want the top," Caroline Bird quotes a group of highly successful women as announcing on the

"Today" show one morning in 1967. "We just want to be near the top and have the fun."

On sex:

. . . the evidence is lying all about, unmistakable. Women Liberationists do not wish to be free to bestow themselves sexually upon men. In being so, they have lost the sense of their peculiar womanly power to control the terms of the relations between themselves and men, and have in exchange for that sense of power received nothing of any truly central value to them. In pronouncing men to be the enemy, they are expressing the wish to return to that state in which, or so they imagine, men *were* the enemy—the fabled beasts whose lusts brought women suffering and death—and women were protected by the moral imperative to struggle against them.

On marriage:

A husband's kindnesses and attentions to his wife, along with his concern that she be well housed and well fed and sexually gratified, are, that is to say [according to the feminist interpretation], only the plans from which he means to construct a towering edifice to his own vanity. The Liberationist does not, like an ordinary nagging wife, demand more of such attentions but wishes rather to assert that they are so inadequate as to mean nothing to her. They are not, indeed, attentions to *her* at all but just a deceptive means for eroding her individual freedom. A house nigger after all is someone whose slavery has been made only a tiny bit more palatable but who is supposed to be obligated by this to be all the more slavish.

This mode of standing the marital transaction exactly on its head, of repaying, as it were, kindness with the imputation of evil motive, is no everyday form of complaint. In fact, it resembles nothing so much as the tantrum of a young child who, unable to claim that he has received no parental indulgence, screams all the louder that such indulgence was meant in the first place to dismiss him and that thus his need is even greater than before.

Similar observations have since been made, twice now, by the redoubtable Mr. Gilder, and recently reinforced by Colette Dowling in her book *The Cinderella Complex* —the complex of the title being whatever it is in women that, she says, makes them shrink from freedom and its risks. And, as I have suggested, almost nothing is more certain than the prospect of many more such proclamations in the future.

We are, as everyone knows, in the midst of a swing to the right, and there are few things the right likes better than anthropologically, zoologically, physiologically buttressed arguments on behalf of what its few literate representatives sometimes call "natural law"—which, when it comes to politics, amounts to the doctrine that things are meant to be the way they were, only more so; and which, when it comes to sexual politics, amounts to the doctrine that men are serpents, women are marsupials, and that's that. So we can expect a good deal more of this sort of thing from my favorite character in recent fiction, Buddy Barnes of Tom Lorenz's *Guys Like Us:*

Buddy slid over. "We're talking life here. We're talking men and women and certain ways of doing things. This stuff goes back a long way. It isn't new." He was stabbing his finger into the bar. "We're talking, what—fifty thousand years of recorded history? This stuff came way before Christ. We're talking basics now. You can't change something like this overnight. You don't change the rules in the middle of the game. No way, Jose."

"We're talking basics"—that is the first way of accounting for the everywhere manifest *horror vitae* of modern feminism. It has the virtue of simplicity, of requiring the minimum of adjustment in our inherited understanding of the way things are. William of Ockham would have loved it.

The second way is slightly more nuanced—which means that, for some time to come, it will probably be less appealing. It is simply to observe that old habits die hard, that any group's movement from one ethos to another—America's waves of immigrants are the obvious examples—is accompanied by countercurrents of resistance.

In the case of women, what this means is that many of them are, quite understandably, reluctant to abandon the protections of a known past in order to get the problematical freedoms of an unknown future. Also, a lot of them, just as understandably, find those freedoms unsettling at first. Therefore it is simply of course that the current avatar of resistance to this change should be a woman, and likewise of course that some contemporary feminists should in any number of ways, all of them grist for glib ironists, revert to the standards of their mothers and grandmothers.

This book is a bet placed on that second explanation. I choose, perhaps optimistically, to take the phrase "women's liberation" literally, as designating a movement for expanded freedom—for women and, not incidentally, men as well. I see it as mainly an outgrowth of the Sixties rejection of tribal taboos, especially sexual ones, on the relations between men and women, and I accordingly see the undeniably strong and growing streak of Grundyism in contemporary feminism as a simple case of recidivism, probably inevitable.

Inevitable, but also deplorable, and probably not tolerable for much longer. Feminists committed one damaging blunder at the beginning of their movement by calling the housewives of America *de facto* prostitutes leading lives of degrading servitude—thus alienating much of their natural constituency. Although most feminists have since come around to recanting on that one, it may well be that the current quixotic campaign to reform the male libido will amount to a blunder of the same magnitude, coming at a time when the movement can no longer afford such errors.

Feminism these days obviously needs all the friends it can get. For its own interests, if nothing else, it is past time for the movement to take the "No Boys Allowed" sign off its clubhouse, mainly by ceasing to encourage those of its members who, when men try to join up, stick out their tongues and call them names. As I write this, the most prominent proponent of the Equal Rights Amendment is a man, the most prominent opponent is a woman, and all polls continue to show that the support of men for most feminist causes equals or surpasses that of women. Whatever advantage there may once have been to casting men as the common enemy in order to close ranks has passed. The continuing chorus to the effect that the white male is the cancer of the universe (we'll look at some examples in the following chapter) is no longer just sophomoric and sexist—it threatens to be politically ruinous as well.

In saying this, I have the peculiar sense of stating something at once trite and new. Most people I know—women and men—would probably agree with most of it, and even a few feminists, notably Betty Friedan, have publicly said something similar. But of course Betty Friedan, among the movement's cognoscenti, is known as an Uncle Tom precisely because of such statements. The fact is that according to the public record—the sum total of publications, pronouncements, and actions—what I've just said is going to be anything but obvious to the people generally represented in the books and the broadcasts. I can only conclude that most prominent feminists have lost touch with their constituents, or are representing only their most retrograde impulses.

It was Jonathan Swift who remarked that while individual men might be fine fellows, mankind was one of nature's least appealing creatures. The same relationship seems to obtain, in spades, between individual feminist women and the sisterhood. There are certainly, for instance, scads of bright feminist women—so why are almost all feminist books so desperately dumb? How is it that the movement's representatives have managed to create the nationwide impression that a feminist is a woman who acts like a rude man? Why did my feminist colleagues on the faculty of Hamilton College—to a woman and man brainy individuals not incapable of subtlety or humor—invariably behave like buffoons when acting en masse, dribbling their energy away in campaigns against student pranks, girlie magazines, and other such *chazzerei,* and why is such behavior, from all reports, typical of their counterparts on many other campuses? Why, in her struggle to be considered a person, does the feminist woman so often see fit to publicly imitate a jackass?

If I am right, and there is this wide disparity between what most men and women sympathetic to the cause are thinking and what is emerging from the caucuses, podiums, and printing presses, then this book may strike a few chords and help steel a few resolves. That, anyway, is its main intention. I make no claim to originality; I'm trying to point, not unearth. In fact, my fondest hope is that the reader's reaction will be that someone has finally gotten around to putting between covers what he or she has been thinking for years.

One thing that I, anyway, have been thinking for some time is that it would be nice if someday soon we could say more or less what feminism as a position *is*—as opposed to what it isn't. At the moment, that is impossible.

THE **MYTH** OF THE **MONSTROUS MALE**

I wish that these people would follow the example of Neil's old nemesis, Mrs. Weatherwax, and start drawing a few lines somewhere. Nothing subtle: mainly just a recognition that taking certain positions rules out taking certain others—that antimale hate literature, for instance, has no place in a movement that coined the term "sexism," and that in general the old shibboleths of feminine propriety, even when wrapped in the colors of radicalism, are the exact opposite of what feminism has to be all about.

In this regard, it would be a good thing if feminists finally came to understand what Gilder and Decter made clear to their enemies some time ago: that when you speak of men as a separate and lower breed of animal against whom it behooves you to band together in packs, you are doing what ladies, until recently, have always done; that in so doing you are reverting to traditional type; that such reversion is necessarily an affirmation of innate, irreducible, and politically unignorable differences between the sexes; that such affirmations undermine every victory won or sought by women since the suffragettes. Whatever she may think she is saying, the woman who carries on in the manner of the women discussed in the next chapter is in fact saying that she is just not naturally at home in the sweaty, grubby world of male enterprise; that anatomy is indeed destiny; that all those exemplary eons of human culture and tribes of aborigines and colonies of termites wasn't telling us no lie: Women are designed for the hive, home, or campsite, blissfully breeding away, and the sooner they get this faddish flight from nature out of their systems and return to first principles, the better it will be for all concerned.

Because let there be no mistake: The doctrine of natural law is just death for feminism. Its rhetoric, whether clinical or lyrical, is never far from the talk of the movement's enemies. George Gilder, who says flatly that sex is always for procreation even when the people involved don't think so (on some deep cosmic level, you see) and that women were made for having babies even if some of them, again, don't feel like it (same old cosmic level to the rescue here), is as usual a case study. But even so shrewd a dialectician as Midge Decter cannot refrain from occasionally beating the bongos on behalf of that sort of thing: the driving, thrusting, single-minded male (only thinking of *one thing,* after all), always either swelling or dwindling (this is not a nice thing to point out, but it *has* to be pointed out: The man with whom Midge Decter sleeps every night is, after all, Norman Podhoretz); the receptive, concave, amniotic, moon-tuned female.

This sort of genitalian mythmaking, this apotheosis of cock and cunt into eternal verities inexorably determining our separate courses from cradle to grave, is *the* central superstition against which all feminist ground must be won. That does not mean rejecting or overhauling or even ignoring "nature"—just letting it fend for itself. You do not have to deny the differences in the way men and women experience sex, for instance—the different rates of arousal and all the rest; you simply have to recognize that, based on past evidence, any attempt to extrapolate those differences into codes and laws will be misbegotten and gross. Any feminist line-drawing should begin with ruling such extrapolations out-of-bounds.

Which is just as well, because if one moral has emerged from the ideological boneyards of the last hundred or so years, it is that such talk is always the trademark of political dodoism, or worse. It is always wrong and always stupid. It has been behind social Darwinism (nature is red in tooth and claw and so we should be, too), various strands of racism (we breed horses for purity and so we should do the same for people), and of course all the laws, only recently overturned and still threatening a comeback, for keeping woman in the nest (that's where the mama bird sits, isn't it?).

Those who think such talk is done should take another look. The academic growth industries of sociobiology, genetics, and cultural anthropology can be counted on to keep supplying reductive metaphors for the way people should be to whomever wants them, way into the future. We can expect to hear more about such curious creatures as the wrasse, a species of fish whose females, should they become dominant in the social structure, automatically grow penises and turn into males (thus showing that maleness is a requirement for leadership); more about right-hemisphere thinking and left-hemisphere thinking and which comes naturally to which sex; more about *x* chromosomes and *y* chromosomes; more about the sperm's metaphysical rite of passage as he hustles and elbows his way through that primordial killing ground, the vaginal (gunfight at the O.K.) canal. It will all be nonsense, but seductive nonsense, because many people find it comforting to think of themselves as organs, plants, or animals rather than as those amphibious makers of choices, human beings.

It will be good for everybody to be on guard against this kind of talk, but particularly important for feminists, to whom it is especially poisonous and, from the evidence, especially alluring. That is why it is so disturbing to see so many of them falling, lash, sass, and bustle, for the line all over again. It raises fears that the ERA fiasco may prove to be symptomatic: defeat snatched from the jaws of victory, the most far-reaching liberation movement of the age frittered and blithered away in an access of backsliding.

For almost certainly, that is how feminism is most likely to be done in—not by the bonehead right, who, like the poor, are always with us, but by the half-conscious, half-disguised complicity of feminists with it. The forces of reaction, powerful as they seem at the moment, are not going to be enough to carry off their back-to-hearth-and-home plans without a certain amount of cooperation. The main hope of their opponents remains what it has always been, as voiced by Norman Mailer: "We yet may win, the others are so stupid." Hold that thought, in this winter of discontent. Stupidity in behalf of expediency is no virtue. Worse, in the not-so-long long run, it's not even expedient.

So this book is also meant to be a flag waved in the field, encouraging those who feel the same way to stick to their guns, pausing only to make sure which guns they are. To me, their identity is clear: the continuing liberation of men and women, which has followed, I think logically, from their rejecting the sexual dialectic of bribery and blackmail, and which today ironically is most threatened by some of its own initiators. There are a number of words for what the liberation is from—repression, stereotyping, sexism—but I think my friend Neil has the best word. It is a liberation from the days when a woman had to pretend to be not amused by certain funny things, not excited by certain exciting things, and not conscious of certain obvious things, when half her being was circulating in the real world and the rest in some eternal Howdy Doody show, and when men had to abet and reinforce her in her duplicities. It is a liberation from having to keep up all that foolishness, from pretending to believe what no one with any brains can believe—from, in a word, bullshit.

Neil himself is not optimistic about the prospects for such a liberation. To him, the current state of feminism is just the old story of Bolsheviks kicking out the czar and then setting up shop themselves in the Kremlin: Names and slogans change, but the fields of force remain the same. Yesterday Carry Nation, today Susan Brown-

35

miller; yesterday "take advantage of," today "exploit"; yesterday "beastly," today "sexist"; yesterday the Purity Crusade, today Women Against Pornography. With his usual odious astuteness, Neil affects to see the evidence for this dreary analysis everywhere:

"You have to know how to read the signs. People are always sending out signals, whether they mean to or not, in the way they dress, eat, walk, whatever. Women's clothes are a perfect example. You take a look at women's clothes these days, at the signals being sent out. Start at the bottom, with the shoes. It's a good place to start, because every woman I've known, just about, has had a thing about shoes. Also, it's a good place to start because of all those liberated women who used to go around telling you that fashionable women's shoes were just like Chinese foot-binding—you know, tokens of female mutilation and all—and that as soon as women's consciousness was raised enough they would all start going around in sensible clodhoppers.

"Well, damn near everyone's consciousness has now been raised, and have you noticed the shoes women are wearing these days? How a few years ago they all started getting pointy and strippy and spiky, like they'd been fifteen years or so before? No? Well, you should notice these things.

"And do you notice that none of these women are talking about what those shoes are saying anymore? Because they can't quite get away with blaming it on men this time, and so they don't want us to pay that kind of attention to such things anymore.

"But fair's fair. I can remember when I had to put up with the most amazing theories about what some woman's wardrobe said about my sex, and I've been waiting for years to get my turn. So I will tell you what those pointy little shoes are saying. It has nothing to do with foot-binding this time—no, sir.

"They are saying, 'You mustn't think that the likes of little old us can have anything to do with running, or anything strenuous like that, now.' And do you know why they started saying that? Because at the time people were starting to put two and two together about this equal-pay-for-equal-work action, and starting to say things like, 'If women have opportunity at the prestige jobs, maybe they should also have equal opportunity at the really shit jobs—meaning dirty, manual labor, stuff like being a coalminer or a garbage person.'

"Also they were saying, 'They should also get drafted, if there's a draft. Hell, they should even be sent into combat, if there's a war.' What those shoes were saying back was, 'WHOA, now, not so fast.' They were saying, 'You all wouldn't think of sending delicate little things like *us* into a muddy old battlefield, would you? You wouldn't expect someone walking around on *us* to carry an eighty-pound knapsack on a forced march, would you now?' That's what they were saying.

"Remember the cartridge belts and combat boots these women used to go around in, back before this drafting-women talk got serious? You saw a bunch of liberated women standing around together, it looked like a Pancho Villa army veterans' reunion. Well, big talk. You're not going to see many of them dressing up like make-believe soldiers again until they're pretty damned confident that make-believe is all it is.

"Face it, man. They're no better than us. They want to get the good things, and dump the bad things on the other guy—just like everybody else. Why should you knock yourself out looking for some kind of consistency? You don't expect to find it in the Democratic party, say. Women are people, and people are piggy. Also, they don't change, not in the long run. My nineteen-year-old friend is going to have to keep jumping through any kind of stupid hoops his girlfriend puts up for him in order to keep getting what he wants, which is her sweet poon, because she knows she can make him do it. That's power, and people as a rule don't give up power, even if keeping it means they have to act like weasels.

"For a few great years—our years, Jehovah be praised —the women our age lost their heads, and actually tried living according to their ideals: love and liberation and all. But it didn't take them long to grow into their mothers and housemothers and commence hammering out the old party line all over again. That's what's been going on for these last ten years or so—and unless I'm mistaken, it's just the overture. Mrs. Weatherwax is coming back strong. Everybody's big these days on getting back to their cultural roots—that's another feature of getting older, you know—and the cultural roots of the female sex, my friend, are piety and piffle and let's-pretend. So the worst is definitely yet to come. We are all in for what may well prove to be America's all-time top-of-the-charts golden age of bullshit."

Well, maybe. Still, I'm betting the other way. There are indeed signs all around us, as usual, but as usual they seem to conflict. Maybe Neil is right, and our generation's slide to senescence may bring with it one of those contractions of the spirit that every now and then seem to come over a whole culture. Perhaps in ten or twenty years Neil and I and the few of us left who remember what it was really like—after various revisionist social historians have convinced most of the rest that we spent most of our time having bad trips and raping people— will be in the position of fading old Regency bucks watching sourly, through bloodshot eyes, the ascendancy of their rectitudinous Victorian juniors: Byron lamenting from Venice that "Cant is so much stronger than Cunt nowadays that the benefit of experience in a man who had well weighed the worth of both monosyllables must be lost to a despairing posterity"; Lord Melbourne moping out his last years in his club, waiting vainly for his one-time star pupil, then queen, to call for him.

Myself, I hold the happy view that humbug, once found out, tends to stay found out, provided that every now and then it is reexposed, and provided that those who continue to preach it in new guises are identified for all to recognize.

2

Talking Back

WHEN a female child is passed from lap to lap so that all the males in the room (father, brother, acquaintance) can get a hard-on, it is the helpless mother standing there and looking on that creates the sense of shame and guilt in the child."

What is a man supposed to do in the face of a sentence like this? My first reaction is to turn the page with a grimace, reflecting that there sure are a lot of loonies in the world, some of them writers.

But such responses are inadequate. That sentence is about the male sex, therefore about me; and what its author, who has never met me, is saying is that I am perforce a child molester, though possibly just a covert one. Now I am trying very hard to imagine any statement comparable to this in the annals of hate literature. Suppose it were about a roomful of women? "When a male child is passed from lap to lap so that all the females in the room can . . . grab at his penis," I suppose. Or Jews: "When a Gentile child is passed from lap to lap so that

43

all the Jews in the room can size him up for one of their ritual child murders . . ."—but enough.

The sentence is from Adrienne Rich's book, *Of Woman Born: Motherhood as Experience and Institution,* recipient of enthusiastic reviews from *Newsweek, Saturday Review,* the *Washington Post . . .* "Everyone of woman born should read this book," says the Baltimore *Evening Sun;* and Mr. Bruce Palmer of Washington, D.C., replying to an article of mine in *Inquiry* magazine scorning the scholarship of Kate Millett's *Sexual Politics* and Susan Brownmiller's *Against Our Will,* writes that if those books aren't scholarly enough for me, "let him work with Mary Daly's *Gyn/Ecology* or Adrienne Rich's *Motherhood as Experience and Institution."*

Well, I have worked with them. I have read them. Has he? If so, how did he feel about that sentence? Did he realize it was about *him?*

The sentence quoted above, as it happens, is not originally Adrienne Rich's own, but quoted approvingly by her from an unpublished paper delivered in 1974 to the American Psychological Association by Jean Mundy, Ph.D. (perhaps that's what makes it "scholarly" in Mr. Palmer's eyes—heavy documentation of other people's obscure fatuities). But it is pretty close to the spirit of the whole book; that was why Rich went so far afield (an unpublished paper delivered by an unknown speaker) to gather it in. And anyone who has read Kate Millett, Susan Brownmiller, Andrea Dworkin, Robin Morgan, Kathleen Barry, and, yes, Mary Daly, or any number of obscurer authors working the same vein, knows that Adrienne Rich is far from being on the outer limits of the movement. Never mind about the zanies of the early years—Valerie Solanas shooting Andy Warhol, Ti-Grace Atkinson (remember?), the blueprints for a new urogenital tract surgically altered along ideological lines. Today they seem pretty clearly to have been a last spasm of the counterculture, the female auxiliary of the Yippies and the Weatherpeople. Most feminists would prefer to forget them, as indiscretions of youth. Let them.

Turn instead to what has been coming out over the last five or six years, at an increasing rate, and you will find that Adrienne Rich and Ms. Mundy are front and center. They are right in the mainstream of contemporary feminism (insofar as there is such a thing), as established by sheer echo-power: what the books and articles keep saying over and over, what any man who has talked with feminists has been hearing over and over. Or, anyway, ought to have heard, if he'd been paying attention.

A lot of men obviously haven't been doing that. Some, a minority, are of course hostile to feminism, and make it a point not to hear such things—but even among those sympathetic to the movement, there has obviously been a great deal of not really listening, a great deal of ritualistic nodding and breast-beating and thinking-of-something-else. Because if these men were to really listen, they would find it much harder to keep up their sympathy than they do now.

Let us, for the length of this chapter, imagine what such a man—one who actually takes seriously what these women are saying—would be hearing about himself; and then try to imagine what—assuming he is not ready to accept the logic of such statements and go stick his head in the oven—he might feel like saying back.

He will have heard, first, that he is a rapist—if not according to the law (which, being man-made, is of course hopeless anyway), then a legitimized rapist (married women who have sex with their husbands when they're not in the mood are being raped) or an ocular rapist ("They rape you with their eyes") or an aspiring rapist (all pornography abuses women and therefore equals rape, and all men love pornography) or a verbal rapist (the infamous construction workers and their lunch-hour overtures) or, at the very least, the accomplice of an army of "myrmidon" rapists keeping women in their place, and therefore a rapist-by-proxy.

Also, of course, he has raped Mother Earth (feminists can get Freudian when it suits their purpose); ecology is a feminist issue, too. So is peace, because wars are essentially sybaritic binges indulged in by men for their own profit and pleasure, one of the main pleasures being that during them they get to do a lot of raping.

It goes without saying (but is said anyway) that he is a fascist; what is a fascist, after all, but someone who sees everything as something to rape? (What *is* a fascist, anyway? Does the word mean anything anymore? Would Mussolini know what these people are talking about?)

Being a rapist, he is also a Nazi, a word that is effectively distinguished from "fascist" only in its power to call up certain lurid images. For instance these, from the most recent tome on the subject, Andrea Dworkin's *Pornography: Men Possessing Women:*

The concentration camp woman, a Jew—emaciated with bulging eyes and sagging breasts and bones sticking out all over and shaved head and covered in her own filth and cut up and whipped and stomped on and punched out and starved—became the hidden sexual secret of our time. The barely faded, easily accessible memory of her sexual degradation is at the heart of the sadism against all women that is now promoted in mainstream sexual propaganda.

Then there is this, from Gloria Steinem: "A woman who has *Playboy* in the house is like a Jew who has *Mein Kampf* on the table." And from Judith Bat-Ada: "Hugh Hefner, Bob Guccione, and Larry Flynt . . . are every bit as dangerous as Hitler, Mussolini, and Hirohito." And Kate Millett's history of the "counterrevolution" against feminism beginning with Nazi Germany. And Susan

Brownmiller's thirty-five pages equating nazism with "rapism," which is in turn demonstrated to be the essence of men's attitude toward women. And Marilyn French's mild-mannered husband in *The Women's Room* whose bottom drawer is revealed to contain a secret cache of pornography featuring Nazi men abusing Jewish women —which discovery leads to such conclusions as this:

My feelings about men are the result of my experience. I have little sympathy for them. Like a Jew just released from Dachau, I watch the handsome young Nazi soldier fall writhing to the ground with a bullet in his stomach and I look briefly and walk on. I don't even need to shrug. I simply don't care. What he was, as a person, I mean, what his shames and yearnings were, simply don't matter.

And much, much more in the same vein.

Men equal rapism equals nazism: That, amazingly, is really the number one equation feeding the mills of feminist rhetoric these days. It may or may not have ever been summed up quite this patly, but it has evidently occurred to some of these women (as no doubt it occurred to Hitler) that the stiff-armed Nazi salute was the purest expression of male sexuality, in comparison to which an actual erection is a pretty middling phallic symbol.

Reading all this stuff through, one begins shrewdly to suspect that a number of these women have taken all too literally Sylvia Plath's famous observation that "Every woman adores a fascist," and have accordingly come to repudiate any leanings in themselves to what some of the movement leaders actually call "phallicist" impulses as recidivist and masochistic, a desire for "The boot in the face, the brute/Brute heart of a brute like you."

One feminist work, Elizabeth Gould Davis's *The First Sex,* goes so far as to argue that the modern *Sieg Heil* penis was created in an evolutionary access of aberrant female weakness for that sort of thing:

The wild habits and raw meat diet of the undomesticated males [Davis thinks that only men are natural carnivores] no doubt led to their gradual sexual development—and eventually to their conquest of the matriarchs. For Louis Berman points out that meat-eaters have larger sexual organs than vegetarians, and this development may have proved irresistible to the women. It is thus possible that the women of the old gynocracies brought on their own downfall by selecting the phallic wild men over the more civilized men of their own pacific and gentle world. . . . There is even evidence that it was woman's sexual preference that determined the ultimate size of the male phallus.

It would be delightful to linger in Ms. Davis's feminist *Paradise Lost,* envisioning thousands of generations of women, in spite of themselves, against their better natures, falling for the Wrong Thing over and over again and thus selectively encouraging its impudence, ballooning it by degrees into its present disreputable dimensions; not discovering the snake in the garden, as Genesis has it, but actually *creating* it . . . What an epic could be written from such a premise! But we must pass on, pausing only to note that *The First Sex* is recommended on the reading list of *The First Ms. Reader,* that it is listed on Robin Morgan's select "Germinal" reading list, that its theories about how women have controlled everything since day one but somehow screwed themselves in the process are everywhere in feminist myth. We must pass on because there is, as usual, a contradictory feminist theory, whose only resemblance to its opposite is that, as usual, men don't come out of it looking all that great.

This one says that sexual man became a jackbooted brute not from female manipulation but, on the contrary, from not getting enough of it. Heterosexual sex is all the doing not of women but of men, who, being innately rapacious, have made of it just one of the ways in which they subdue everything in their path. Marriage, with its cult of sexual fidelity, is a male invention designed to keep women in the home, producing babies bearing the father's name; even worse is its opposite, the sexual license that blossomed in the Sixties, since that has the effect of denying women the meager protections they have won for themselves under the old dispensation and throwing them into what has always been a man's world. Both the virgin and the prostitute, wife and "other woman," started as ideas in the male mind, to be imposed on a gullible womankind consequently disabled from developing its own, natural, sexual inclinations, which are, of course, for love. It is no coincidence that "masculinist" terms for sexual intercourse like "fuck" and "bang" convey violent dominance, because that is exactly what men have turned sex into.

If I were a woman, there's no question which of the two stories I would prefer. The Davis version portrays woman as a queen in exile, struggling to regain the rightful sovereignty that she had yielded in a (very) protracted moment of generous but unwise indulgence. Variations of this account keep cropping up in the literature, but unquestionably the second, really nasty, one has prevailed. And that story, from a woman's point of view, is one of endless, hopeless horror: rape-rape-rape, fuck-fuck-fuck; clitoridectomies and infibulations and foot-bindings; menstruating women locked in huts; feebleminded women burned as witches; women in childbirth racked and gouged; generations of women herded into homes like Jews into showers, there to be beaten by drunken brutes and killed with childbearing, the unmarried residue wasting away as derided supernumeraries in convents, mills, or, at best, the cold extra rooms of inhospitable homes. "If you want a picture of the future," Winston Smith is told in Orwell's *1984,* "imagine a boot stamping on a human face—forever." There are plenty of women around these days who will tell you that, for them, that is already a picture of their past.

There is of course no question that all those things happened, in many places still are happening. The vast majority of people have always, by any humane standard, lived awful lives, and women have had their portion of the misery, up to the present; of the hundred million or so people violently put to death in this century, many, though by no means half, have been women. That is not the question. The question is whether the source of all this pain is specifically male nature rather than human nature (or conditioning, or whatever), and whether women have been its special victims—whether history has indeed been one long horror story of male Nazis and female Jews.

An awful lot of feminist polemic amounts to a tunnel-vision survey of history's atrocities, the moral being that, yes, women have been singled out for victimization. It is a method available to anyone who wants to get mad. Give me some time and the services of a genealogical society and I will prove to you that history reveals a pattern of systematic violence against Gordons, going back to my family's origins in Scotland—first with the depredations of whatever clan our clan feuded with, then on to Culloden and the bloody British, then a tour through the industrial nightmare and up to the casualties of our own calamitous century. It's easy—just a matter of leaving everybody else out of the picture. To read Susan Brownmiller on the Second World War, for instance, is to forget for a time that the Germans and Russians ever got around to actually killing any men, so busy seem they to have been with the women.

By leaving everybody else out of the picture, feminists

have put together a number of histories designed to show that the past is one long story of male jackboot coming down on female face, fitfully illumined by upwellings of female resistance.

We are repeatedly reminded of witch-burnings because they constitute the sole recorded instance of female victims of capital punishment outnumbering male victims; we are not, of course, reminded of the many cases (for instance Salem) where witches were convicted mainly on the testimony of other women; we are likewise allowed to believe, against all available evidence, that women had no part in the trials or executions, or in the moral climate that brought them about.

We are reminded of Joan of Arc, burned by men, but not of the hundreds of men burned by (Bloody) Mary Tudor, nor of the hundreds of thousands of other martyred heretics who, not being women, are ideologically impertinent.

We are shown evidence that male doctors over the ages have been responsible for the deaths of untold women in labor, through ignorance or the indiscriminate application of medical technology. And of course it's true: Up until quite recently, doctors have almost certainly killed more people than they've cured, including for instance George Washington (if it had been Martha, we'd never hear the last of it), and the statistics on unnecessary surgery indicate that even today many doctors, both male and female, are disinclined to leave well enough alone.

Speaking of medical women, Florence Nightingale of course puts in an appearance, fighting off the male chauvinism of the British medical establishment, ministering to the wounded of Balaklava. But there is a curious averting of the eyes from the hospital itself, full of mutilated humans, all of them male, suffering and dying because of the military adventurism of their female monarch.

Queen Victoria does, to be sure, show up as part of another exhibit. Like Catherine the Great and Elizabeth I and Isabella of Spain, she demonstrates what exemplary rulers women can be when given the chance. But we are not encouraged to linger very long on this particular display, since to do so might be to recall Elizabeth's genocidal campaign against the Irish, Catherine's role in the partition of Poland, Isabella's expulsion of the Jews, or Victoria's ferocious militarism. Listen, for instance, to Victoria writing to Disraeli: "The Queen is really distressed at the low tone which this Country is inclined to hold [she means its reluctance to go to war]. . . . Oh, if the Queen were a man, she would like to go and give those Russians . . . such a beating!" (They did, which was why Florence Nightingale became necessary.)

If, recalling episodes like those, we remark that women rulers have if anything been an especially bloody-minded bunch, we will be told that it's not their fault but the fault of their male advisers, or anyway of their culture, or anyway *something* with men in it, forcing them into the aggressive masculine mold. (Similarly, Susan Brownmiller will explain to you that female inmates who rape other inmates with broom handles are really only imitating men.)

That would have come as news to Victoria's advisers, who spent much of their time trying to restrain their queen's wilder plans for the conquest of everything in sight. It would have seemed a very strange account of events indeed to those cavaliers goaded into joining the Second Crusade by Eleanor of Aquitaine, contemptuously throwing distaffs to the shirkers ("Oh, if the Queen were a man . . .") and leading her contingent of Amazons to glorious disaster in the Holy Land. Zoologists will perhaps wonder how the female shell duck, who habitually demands that her mate attack every other male in range and abandons him if he doesn't, has been forced

into this obnoxious practice by male influence. And
American males recalling from their high-school days the
program of selectively administered sexual rewards
through which they were encouraged by women to bash
their bodies against one another in weekly combat, on
the football field or in some other arena, will perhaps
doubt that it was the men who rigged the whole business,
the women who were brainwashed.

All the same, the old idea that women are naturally
exempt from bloodlust continues and thrives, held back
from the wastebasket to which other such ideas have
been consigned. Feminists want to believe it, and so does
everyone else. *I* would like to believe it. That gentle man
W. H. Auden, echoing many another, looked forward to
the day when males would be relieved of the "phallic
toys" of warfare, and all international affairs would be
turned over to women, "preferably married ones." Who
would not endorse such a plan? Except that the women,
for instance Margaret Thatcher and Indira Gandhi, turn
out to be rather fond themselves of those phallic toys.

Above all, feminists want to believe it, even when the
evidence to the contrary is hitting them in the face. The
feminist interviewer Oriana Fallaci, for instance, who has
pierced through the fronts of more powerful men than
you could shake a phallic toy at, only to frisk like a puppy
at the feet of Indira Gandhi, woke up one morning to
discover that her hero had abolished the Constitution
and thrown the opposition into jail. To her credit, she
searched her soul. In *Interview with History* she says:
". . . it was impossible to be a woman and not feel
redeemed, vindicated, by her enormous success, which
belied all the banalities used to justify patriarchy and
male rule in any society. Being a woman, justifications of
her wrongs came much easier."

In other words, it was just as Indira's opponent, M.
Moraji Desai, had told her: "Had Indira Gandhi been a

man, the world would have realized at once she was a fascist." And even worse: ". . . considering too the complicity that exists between you women, you didn't notice her fascist mentality."

For a few moments, Oriana Fallaci brought herself to consider this earthshaking possibility—that the word "woman" could belong in the same sentence with the word "fascist." For a few moments. Then the complicity of which Desai spoke began to reassert itself:

She has beautiful hazel eyes, a little sad, and a strange, indulgent [indulgent!], enigmatic smile that awakens curiosity. . . . In that sense [the sense that she's a woman] I'm still on the side of Indira. My refusal of the woman as politician is not accompanied by my refusal of the woman as such. Even during the hours that followed the arrest of the opposition leaders and her coup, that is even during the burst of my indignation against her, I couldn't help thinking how alone she was and how much more unhappy than a man [like Nixon?] who puts himself in the same situation.

What we have here, ladies and gentlemen, is woman's intuition, another cliché that feminists are reluctant to discard. In this case it is telling our correspondent that while other, male, international thugs who try their enigmatic smiles on her are lying through their teeth, Mrs. Gandhi, with her hazel eyes, wasn't, at least not on some level. Some intuitive level. We have male leaders invading countries and planning assassinations not to expand or secure their power but because, being men, they like doing such things, guns being (Freud again!) simply masculine extensions and so forth and so on. We have female rulers doing exactly the same things, but only out of painful necessity and against their natures, and all the while feeling much more sensitive, more *unhappy* about it than men. Above all, we have an essentially hormonal theory of history, a testosteroniad, coming from people who will then tell you that anyone who suggests that women are hormonally programmed is a male chauvinist genetic-determinist reactionary pig. And we have a steadfast, steely-eyed refusal to consider the most obvious reason for the pretty much equal distribution of atrocities between male and female leaders: that nations never have as much land or power or wealth or security as they would like; and that anyone entrusted with enacting national will is frequently tempted to do atrocious things, regardless of hormonal makeup.

Well, then, what, on the simplest level, might a not altogether mesmerized man say to this sequence of charges that he is a fascist, Nazi, rapist, and, in general, the source of everything wrong with everything?

What, to begin with, does one do with the assertion that there is an elemental connection between maleness and Naziness? (Ignore it, ideally, as beneath contempt, and wait for it to go away. But it hasn't, and some of the mud has stuck.)

There are two basic lines of available refutation: (1) Remind people of men who have not been Nazis (Wolfgang Amadeus Mozart, Willie Mays, Confucius, Robert Fulton, Pope Leo XIII); (2) remind people of Nazis who have not been men—of Leni Riefenstahl (Kate Millett will probably tell you that she illustrates how female artists have been forced to sacrifice their talents to male values . . .); of Ilse Koch, infamous doyenne of Buchenwald and alleged inventor of the epidermal lampshade (Adrienne Rich may argue that such inventions show a glimmer of maternal nest-building instinct, being after all domestically useful and decorative . . .); of the female camp guards; of the thousands of women at the rallies roped off into separate sections because their enthusiasm

for *Kontaktsucht* with the Führer so dramatically surpassed that of the men; of the scores—their numbers
exceeding their male counterparts by about two to one
—who committed suicide on hearing of his death (Susan
Brownmiller will explain: They were terrified of being
raped by the Russians, the Russians were notorious for
their raping . . .); and of the fact that Hitler was one of
the first German leaders elected after the enactment of
woman suffrage, and that he himself gave women credit
for most of his early success.

Will that do it? I would like to think so, because this
kind of childish vileness makes me feel like taking a bath,
and I begin to understand in my bones why no man
before me has taken on himself the onus of slinging any
of this kind of shit back.

But, no, that probably won't do; we are, after all,
dealing in ideological essences, to which examples of
actual people can always be made to seem trivial. Nor
will it, probably, do any good if I myself note, for instance, that my father risked his life for four years
fighting the Nazis, and that about a fourth of his millions
of male colleagues died doing the same. That's all John
Wayne fantasy, just glamorizing the real fact of one
bunch of men with guns facing another bunch of men
with guns, some of them wearing swastikas but all of
them loving it, because (Andrea Dworkin again) "men
especially love murder." Also, it's masculinist history,
leaving out the rape victims of Budapest and Rosie the
Riveter—poor martyred Rosie, forced to sweat away in
the factories while her man was out painting the town in
Normandy and Iwo Jima, then forced out of the factories
when he came staggering back, like some drunk husband
at three in the morning, and selfishly demanded his job
back.

And the same goes for the equation of maleness and
rape: It does no good for me to say that *I* never raped

anyone and am just about positive that I would be physically incapable of doing it to save my life. "There's no satisfaction for a man, unless a woman shares it," says Aristophanes' Lysistrata. She's absolutely right about that. Isn't one big feminist complaint that women have had to fake orgasms all these years just to keep their men happy? How is that supposed to square with this other theory that what really turns men on is making women suffer, that we get some kick out of knowing that we're feared and loathed by the person in our arms?

The men reading this will think that what I'm about to say is insultingly obvious, but, believe me, it will, from the evidence, come as news to some of your women friends. Speaking for myself, I have never sought to induce fear and loathing in any woman to whom I have been attracted. At the times when I suspected that my presence was about to cause even tremors of loathing in the beloved, I invariably became morose and withdrawn. I know that rape does occur, mainly among the poor (in America it is committed by blacks about five times as often as it is by whites, a fact that I would someday like to see explained by those who call it a logical extension of political and economic power), as I know that there are people who drink their own urine or stick bones through their noses, but it is not something that I can easily come to understand introspectively. Honest. ("*Why are you getting so defensive?*" *Because I've been called a Nazi rapist child molester, that's why.*)

In any case, rapists are not my brothers or colleagues, and they are certainly not, as Susan Brownmiller calls them, my "myrmidons," since a myrmidon (Brownmiller helpfully explains this for me) is someone who does what you want him to, and if rapists were to do what I wanted them to, they would all take ship for some distant deserted island and never come back. What, after all, are they supposed to be doing for me? A certain considerable portion of my life has been devoted to getting along as well as possible with this woman or that; and as far as I can see, the simple fact that rapists exist has, by creating undertones of fear and suspicion toward all men, only made that harder. Also, of course, the sort of men who rape women are often the same sort who rob and stab the likes of me.

Ah, but even assuming that I've been telling the truth here, how about the subconscious? What a useful concept it is, the subconscious, for those who want to tell you what you are really like. (And how persistently that old Sigmund Freud, kicked out the feminist front door because of his nasty penis-envy talk, keeps sneaking in through the back door.) Well, what can one say? By definition, my subconscious is something I can't talk about. Perhaps it wants to do terrible things to women, and perhaps in that way the world's slashers and flashers are its myrmidons, rampaging around like Walter Pidgeon's Krellian mind-projections in *Forbidden Planet.* Monsters from the id! If so, that's a good reason for its staying *sub,* where it belongs. I hold myself accountable for keeping it in its place—but not for someone else's theory about what it would like to do if let out of the cage, and certainly not for some subliminal primate code by which it is supposedly telegraphing marching orders to the legions of rapists that my poor old deluded conscious really thinks it wishes were in jail.

Nor am I prepared to sit still for the theory that if I view women as sex objects, as I certainly sometimes do, I am participating in a kind of cultural accommodation to rape, which is just the ultimate objectification . . . and so forth and so forth.

In the past when I looked at someone as a sex object, it was generally with the hope that she might come to consider me in the same way, and rape had nothing to do with it, in fantasy or in fact, one way or the other. On the occasions when my feelings were returned and things wound up where the old sex-objectification business tends to lead them—that is, to two people humping happily away—I may have (getting as close as I can to the subconscious now) at times felt like—what? A Chinook salmon churning upstream? A boat rocking on the ocean? (*God,* this is embarrassing!) Anyway, never, so help me God, like Rommel driving deep into Egypt. It wasn't until Kate Millett came along that the thought even occurred to me.

What was going through the woman's mind I can't say. It was none of my business, after all. Maybe *she* was thinking of panzers and boots, and maybe at such moments some men do too. There is certainly evidence that some members of both sexes enjoy rape fantasies and suchlike, though no evidence whatsoever, *pace* a lot of loose talk, that the women have had such nasty-mindedness beaten into them by the men, to whom it comes naturally.

Anyway, so what? A fantasy is a fantasy by virtue of its dissociation from reality. That some women swoon over Rhett Butler or Heathcliff is a fact not likely to make your average nondemented male confuse himself with either. Should such delusions come upon him, chances are he need only consult the mirror, or his bankbook, or contemplate the consequences from the women in his life were he to start doing a Tarzan number. If anything, in fact, he is likely to feel exactly the way many women feel when comparing themselves to male sexual fantasies: inadequate, confused (Is *that* what they want?), more than a little resentful.

All of the above may seem—in fact unquestionably is —pretty simpleminded: women calling men Nazis and thugs; a man calling them Nazis and thugs back. I include it because I think men have been forbearing for too long, and that it would be a good thing if certain women were to get an idea of what it would be like if some men were to pay them back in kind.

Of course, not all feminists are as relentlessly obtuse as Rich, Brownmiller, Steinem, and Dworkin, and even some of those sympathetic to the premises of such women are capable of modulating, at times, into something more reasonable and persuasive. At such times, they will talk less about boots stomping faces than about subtle and pervasive influences working covertly rather than overtly. The main assumption—that society is a hierarchy in which men tell women what to do—remains the same, but the focus is less on rape (although one hears, occasionally, about the "mind-rape" of television and suchlike) than on unspoken compacts and messages, particularly as promoted in the media. In fact the media, more often than not, with its assumed power to control everyone's view of the world, is the main target.

The most popular term for the array of noncoercive processes by which men are believed to control women's lives is "patriarchal conditioning." My own view of patriarchal conditioning is that it doesn't exist out of proportion to other kinds of conditioning, particularly matriarchal—that women are what men have made them no more than men are what women have made them. Much of the rest of the book will be spent arguing this point. Right now, it seems only fair to listen to what a feminist not hopelessly given over to rant and bile might say on behalf of such women and their argument that men are rapists and fascists and Nazis, by way of answering back to the above defense and counterattack. The following is my best guess at what one of them—I'll call her Mira—might like to say back:

"You may actually be as big a gold-plated sweetie as you say you are, and there may be others like you, sensi-

tive souls sitting at home drinking sherry and listening to
Vivaldi. I even think I may have met a few, most of them
gay. But because of your sex you have been shielded
from a few ugly facts that women have to deal with all
the time.

"Not all of the men we go out with try to take advantage of us sexually—try to bully or bribe or wheedle their
way into our beds so they can put another notch on the
belt and dump us to go after another target—but a lot of
them do. Some of us would say most of them. Not all of
the men we meet socially or see on the street make us feel
like pieces of meat, but a lot of them do, and a lot of the
others, like you for instance, seem to expect a great deal
of credit for treating us as human beings.

"You can make all the fun you want of the feelings
many of us have that on some level most men expect us
to enjoy being raped and they therefore don't think it's
a big deal. I confess that, not being a mind reader, I don't
know exactly what level it is. The fact remains that all of
us have been hearing that kind of talk all our lives, mainly
from men. We've also heard about the law-school classes
where a male professor has a male student poke a pencil
at a circle drawn on a moving piece of paper, thus proving that a woman can't be penetrated against her consent.
Some of us have been present in police stations where
rape cases are handled according to that peculiar theory.
Some of us have taken a look at the hardcore pornography that likes to show women being raped and loving it
—and frankly, what we see there makes us wish at times
that we were the female sex of some other species.
(We've also heard about the "snuff" movies, where a
woman is actually murdered before the camera so that
the patrons can get a final kick. Perhaps you can explain,
when you feel like it, how that's so different from what
went on at Auschwitz.)

"We can't help but notice the connection between

what we've seen there and the way women are represented in the media generally. And we've gone on to notice the connection between the way we're shown in the media and the way we're treated in the office, on the street, and in the home. Do you want to hear the statistics on battered wives? Do I have to go on?

"In spite of all your pooh-poohings, my man, you, even you, *know* that in every way you can think of, women are represented and treated as objects, to be enjoyed, exploited, and discarded. I may not have an answer to chicken-and-egg questions about which kind of abuse causes which—whether stereotypes in the media produce roles in life more than the other way around; whether women are economically powerless because of psychological dependency or vice versa. Unlike you, however, I'm not moved to ridicule the people who are trying to sort it all out. No doubt some of them have come up with some shaky, one-sided, even crazy theories, and no doubt some of the theories contradict one another. At least they're trying. When was it ever different in new fields of study? And woman's study *is* a new field because people like you, as far as your actions showed, were quite content with the old legends and lies.

"Which leads me to the subject of you and your little monsters from the id. Very cute. Congratulations on not being a rapist. I'm delighted to hear that your subconscious wouldn't hurt a fly. But that's not the point. The point is the consciousness, of you and other men, as acted out in the society we all have to live in. I'm afraid it could still do with some—you should excuse the expression—raising. I'm frankly a little tired of men—and you're scarcely the first, you know—saying how much they deplore sexism and job discrimination. (You haven't said that? Well, *do* you deplore them? . . . You do. Thought so. Do you deplore interrupting people, too?)

"As I was saying, I'm tired of hearing about how all you liberal men deplore these things. Look around you. It seems pretty obvious that you're not deploring it enough. Or, since I don't want to hurt your sensitive male ego—and I'm sort of tired of hearing about that, too —let's just say that fellows like you are obviously princes among the toads and God's gift to liberated women, but that you'll have to excuse me while I go handle some of the problems caused by all those other men."

Mira's speech is, to the best of my recollection, an accurate distillation of what one hears in arguments on the subject. Even thus filtered, it seems to me pretty compelling.

There's no question in my mind that if I had been born female, I would, at least for a time, have been a radical feminist, quite possibly of the most misanthropic sort. When I was a child, nothing irritated me so much as being treated according to an adult's-eye view of children: the sweet old ladies talking baby talk to you, the degrading menus with special dishes for "little skippers." I remember feeling especially murderous toward the cute little freckles-cowlick-and-missing-front-tooth excrescences that used to decorate Kellogg's cereal boxes. So it's not hard to understand why many women, contemplating the generations of their foremothers who have gone through their entire lives as "girls," just *hate* the Barbie-doll-to-Bunny *shtik* and the men who (they assume) have sold it to them.

All the same, I'm not a woman; and the more I see and hear of these people, the less inclined I am to apologize for that fact, or to tolerate, just because to some degree I can understand its sources, the *confiture* of demagoguery, bogus scholarship, cheap shots, and spite that many feminists today call "feminist theory." I have

63

finally figured out that there is no point engaging in a dialogue the issue of which turns out to be, when are you going to stop being a Nazi? I recommend this revelation to other men. It is, as they say, liberating. They can get mad; you can get mad.

So, without for the moment going into the finer points of the issue, I would like to imagine, once again, what I, an unapologetic male, staying pretty much on Mira's level and feeling no chivalric compunctions about giving tit for tat, might say back. I might sound like this:

First of all, Mira, let's clear up a simple matter of fact. You mentioned snuff movies. *There are no snuff movies.* The FBI tore the pornography industry apart looking for one, because, like you people, it desperately wanted there to be one, but without success. And you, my dear, either don't know what you're talking about when you drag them in, or don't care, or think that because you're oppressed and sincere and getting in touch with your anger you should be indulged a bit when it comes to things like mere facts. Well, sorry. By the old rules— according to which women were in tune with truths deeper than mere facts, and ladies were never admitted to be in the wrong—you would have been indulged. But the rules have been changed, at your insistence, and fair's fair.

Well then. As for the rest. I make no claims to any special sensitivity to either the male or female lot. But I *have* looked around, as you urge, and picked up a few things that you seem to have missed. I can understand why you get angry at the cultural depictions of women; as I said, I felt somewhat the same way as a child. But I don't feel that way anymore, because at some point— about the point, probably, when I faced the fact that I would always hate football—I started figuring out that the cereal boxes and TV commercials didn't necessarily have anything to do with me.

It was a rough period—it is called, usually, "adolescence"—but in the long run, things seem to have turned out rougher for the men, many of them now grease monkeys or army lifers or potbellied jocks with molting crew cuts, who chose not to make such adjustments. I can see now, looking back, that it was rough for the girls my age as well (neither sex made it any easier for the other), and that the pain was compounded by the way each sex tended to evaluate the other, as well as itself, according to the prevailing sexual orthodoxy.

Anyway, that's all blood under the bridge now. Few of us pass unscarred through that period; but from what I can see, there are today many adults, both men and women, capable of inhabiting without trauma a world whose expressed idea of what they should be is often at odds with their own. Why aren't you one of them? Why do you *care* about what the media, the television commercials and all the rest have to say about your sex? (*I* don't lose any sleep over the little Ti-D Bowl yachtsman in the toilet.) Don't you ever feel a little silly monitoring the kid stuff of our culture? A cartoon from a 1969 *New Yorker:* an indignant congressman standing at his desk, saying, "Mr. Chairman, I rise to refute the Smothers Brothers." That was a *joke.* Don't you recognize yourself in it? "Madame Cochairperson, I rise to speak in the matter of the Barbie Doll." Whence this unseemly lust for the chickenshit? Grow up.

You may say (you said something like it) that you need to pay attention to such things because they affect your life in all ways. Spell them out. You mean economically? Even Ronald Reagan, for Christ's sake, believes in equal pay for equal work. The problem there is not the media but a traditional economic convention that both of us agree should be changed, and is being changed.

Do you mean because of the "rape culture" that the media supposedly expresses and promotes, objectifying

women and all that? Since when is vulnerability to violence restricted to women? In the 1960s, when my hair
was long in the fashion of the time, I was regularly
harassed and threatened by the same construction-
worker types that have today taken such a prominent
place in feminist demonology. It was scary, especially
when others like me, mostly male, were being clubbed
and shot by the *Lumpenproletariat,* whose symbol, the
hard hat, so charmed the president of the United States
that he put one on for the cameras.

But it did not occur to me to draw any ideological
conclusions beyond the obvious one: that the type of
people who drop out of high school tend to envy the type
of people who go to college; that for good reasons the
resentment is especially strong among manual laborers,
most of whom are men; and that sometimes the expression of those feelings can become violent. Insofar as they
are expressing hostility rather than pathetic efforts at
friendliness, the construction workers who ogle and
smirk at the stylish young women passing their meals-on-
wheels are saying what years ago they were saying to me:
that compared to them I had it soft, and it made them
mad. The reason they feel that way is that it is the truth.
You don't want to hear that, because much of your cher-
ished indignation depends on a belief that those poor
slobs are your oppressors. But they aren't, and they
aren't the "myrmidons" of your oppressors either.

In fact, a good deal of feminist double-talk comes from
a vaguely sensed anomaly that it would be unpleasant to
face directly: that while theoretically it is a liberation
movement, full of antielitist rhetoric, in actuality it is in
many cases a rebellion of the upper middle class against
the lower middle class. Just that.

In feminist melodrama, the main distinction between
male characters and female characters is that the latter
obviously have college educations and the former do not.

66

The male characters drink beer, talk loud, say "har-har" a lot, and are fond of truck-stop idioms ("jugs," "baby"); the women read books, speak in complete sentences, and dress with stylish understatement. It ought to be the stuff of a harmless class-conflict comedy, like "The Odd Couple." But not with you. You dislike these people with the natural aversion that cultured people often feel for the underbred.

Fine. I feel the same way about the street kids who keep tearing the aerial off my car. But because your leftish brand of romanticism won't allow you to feel hostile to your social inferiors, you have to generalize the enemy into something you can think of as an oppressor class—men. So you come up with this Tinkertoy "myrmidon" theory about how all the male boors you've ever met are in secret league with the nonboors, then close your eyes and throw a tantrum, or "express your rage," or "get in touch with your feelings," or whatever you want to call it. Whatever term you choose, what it amounts to is turning up the car radio so that nobody can hear the knocking under the hood.

Finally, you may say that you are forced to pay attention to the media representation of women because of its influence, which affects you whether you like it or not. What sort of influence? "Pervasive" influence, you say. Influence that is "everywhere." Turning off the television and reading Henry James is all very well, you say (your voice rising), but the fact remains that you have to live your life in a society whose average member spends about as much time watching television as working. How can I be so pigheaded as to ignore such a potent force?

Maybe I'm misjudging you. Maybe you wouldn't say anything quite so trite. In any case, many of your sisters do, all the time. As I say this, the latest issue of *Ms.* leads off with an article by Gloria Steinem, calibrating the meaning for women of media-star popularity polls: Alan

Alda is up (good), but so is Clint Eastwood (bad). Or here's another one, Kathleen Barry, in the recent book *Female Sexual Slavery:* "These practices are woven into the fabric of culture and as such they give cultural sadism its own evolution and history and support it by an ideology that legitimizes and supports it." Typical here are the mushy metaphors: an evolutionary fabric supporting an ideology; everything, almost, but the old all-purpose explainer of how ideas work their influence, "in the air."

It is, of course, just a variant of the trendiest platitude of the day: that everything we aren't proud of inside our heads was put there by the media. The language recalls 1950s campaigns against fluoridated water and reds under beds, or analogies to radiation poisoning and invasions of body snatchers—little pods being planted between the ears of a nation narcotized by video rays. Even the old Vance Packard hobgoblin, "subliminal perception," has been resuscitated from the Fifties: A popular paperback book on the subject, Wilson Bryan Key's *Subliminal Seduction,* displays on its cover an advertisement for some drink, featuring a glass full of ice cubes, and asks: "ARE YOU BEING SEXUALLY AROUSED BY THIS PICTURE?" (No. Next question?)

Splice this truism—that we are all pawns of the media —with a second—that no woman is to blame for anything bad about herself—and you have the major strain in contemporary feminism, promoted by women who find it strangely comforting to depict themselves as Jews in camps. It may all be true in one sense: The person who tells you that the media has undermined his or her capacity to think is at least demonstrating that *something* has. Otherwise, it is simply an abject plea to be absolved from free will.

The fact is that if you don't like the media, you can, to a great extent, avoid it: Throw away your TV set and replace your car radio with a tape deck with your own set

68

of cassettes; buy books instead of magazines; go hiking or partying; eschew people who want to talk about soap operas, football games, and designer-jeans ads and cultivate people who want to talk about other things; go out and get drunk or stoned or laid, or stay in and listen to music or read or meditate or cook or have kids and play with them: Live a life of your own, in short. Who's stopping you?

If you can't bring yourself to do these things, don't blame your spinelessness and lousy taste on others. Don't try to blame me, in particular, or the male sex in general for the female stereotype that you find so obnoxious. *I* never bought a Barbie doll when I was a kid. *Cosmopolitan* and *Vogue,* Yves St. Laurent and Gloria Vanderbilt haven't made their millions catering to the whims of my sex, which, if it had been consulted in the matter, would have frozen women's fashions in 1969, golden age of the miniskirt. It wasn't we who twenty years ago made Gloria Steinem into a Bunny; she did it herself. It's time for her, and you, to stop taking all that out on us.

You should stop, if for no other reason, because there is something very degrading in claiming that one's capacity for free thought has been overcome by the likes of Betty Crocker and Bill Blass. It is like losing one's head at a Ripple party; it is like being seduced by David Eisenhower. It is nothing that any adult should ever admit to. If women have really had their sense of self wiped out by such things, then they have the self-reliance and intelligence of lobotomized white rats, and it was clearly a mistake to give them the vote; hell, they should be kept in cages and fed pellets through the bars.

You may say that, because of the role forced on women in a patriarchal society, they are more susceptible than men to such influences. Actually, it should be just the reverse. Women have traditionally been raised to be more, not less, skeptical than men toward the blandishments of others—the lover-men who want their bodies and the salesmen who want their money. If a woman lets the media tell her how to live, it's because she chooses to.

So much for the back-and-forth over whom to blame for whatsoever women find less than inspiring in themselves. One thing at least that both sides agree on is that, whosoever's work it may be, women have so far seemed to be more susceptible than men to the influence of others, that as a group they still seem to pay more attention to others' ideas of what they should be like—not just to the media, which is for morons, but above all to one another. The rise of the "women's movement" just confirms that observation; it is impossible to imagine anything comparable for men.

"In America," wrote Cyril Connolly thirty-five years ago in *The Unquiet Grave,* "all the women have their set of girl-friends; some are cousins, the rest are gained at school. These form a permanent committee who sit on each other's affairs, who 'come out' together, marry and divorce together, and who end as those groups of active, healthy, well-informed club-women that govern society."

From what I can see, it's as true as ever. Behind the caricature of an endlessly chatting womankind branching into grapevines and bunching into cliques, there has been at least one truth: Women have always talked to one another more than men are likely to, and certainly have listened to one another more. Women as a group just seem to care more about what others think of things and people, including themselves. In a way which can baffle men, they tend to see themselves as part of a community of evolving, shared values, where an opinion is less a flag to wave than something for measurement, comparison, and possibly adjustment. Inevitably, "individualism" has become a bad word in the language of feminist theory.

It would be silly—though of course it's done all the time—to say that this particular difference redounds to the credit of either sex, to say either that men are self-involved monologists while women are sensitive and responsive, or that men are self-reliant freethinkers while women are camp followers. It would be fruitless to try to determine whether women's characteristic dependency on social opinion was at some primordial epoch chosen as a matter of preference or resorted to because of a more elemental dependency on men, requiring as it would (wheels within wheels) the further determination of to what extent *that* dependency was initiated or imposed, and so on. These issues invariably recede unprofitably into the unpublished past.

The important thing is to acknowledge that now women are, for the most part, justified in considering themselves as free as men to reject such dependencies as they find irksome. And if they want to be serious about such rejections, they can begin by repudiating sisterhood, and all such calls to individual self-abnegation on behalf of consensus. They can do what, manifestly, none of the women writers cited in the course of this chapter have chosen to do: switch off that little parrot in the back of the brain, and think for themselves.

Hard to see how that can come about, though, if we all decide that traditional femininity is something women have been suckered into over the millennia. What misogynist ever made a charge so severe? How can men sympathize with, or women take heart from, the spectacle of an entire sex buying the same bill of goods generation after generation? Lobsters, reportedly, will keep getting caught in pots over and over until they finally reach the right size for eating—but then, lobsters are notoriously obtuse. Not even Saint Jerome, or any of his antifeminist brethren, thought women were obtuse. In that opinion, modern feminists stand alone.

The fact, of course, is that women *aren't* especially obtuse. As my friend Mira says, look around you. You will see smart men and stupid men, smart women and stupid women, the ratio being about the same for both sexes. You can tell the stupid ones because they are the people saying stupid things—things that don't make sense, that don't check out, that contradict. So far so good. Now for the boggler. The women saying the stupid things are doing it from exactly the same cause as the men: stupidity.

See that woman over there, Andrea Dworkin? Her problem is *not* that she was raised to play with dolls. (So was Mary McCarthy.)

Notice that one in the corner, Kate Millett, the one cutting snippets out of books she doesn't like, then cropping and framing them so as to make them seem to say what she wants them to have said? Such mendacity is not, normally, the inevitable consequence of having been raised in pink dresses. (Richard Nixon never wore pink dresses.)

And as for Adrienne Rich over there, grabbing that girl baby from its father's arms and telling him to "unhand her, you pervert"—whatever her affliction may be, most women have managed to grow up without contracting it.

Let us face it: There is just something wrong with those people, something entirely apart from their sex. Their sex enters into it in only one way: People are listening to them because they are women. They are the inheritors of the traditional dispensation that permits women to whine and weep and talk nonsense to an extent not granted most men. Except that, at the same time, they say they want something completely contradictory—to be taken seriously, listened to critically.

Fine. That means, first of all, cutting down drastically on the allowance for blithering and blubbering. It is time for men who claim sympathy with feminism to do just that. It should be recognized that making allowances for nonsense just because women are talking it is paternalism, of the most venerable kind. If we're serious about this, then it won't do to listen sympathetically as Robin Morgan or Susan Brownmiller informs you that the world would be a nicer place without you. Sympathy in such cases is condescension, dating from the days when women were not to be thought of in certain ways— neither as doctors and scholars nor as demagogues and fatheads. The last twelve years have demonstrated once and for all a woman's right, and capacity, to make anything she wants out of herself, including a fool. Congratulations, ladies.

3

Mira Redux:

A Conversation and

a Conclusion

WHEN I was a child, I used to have arguments with my sister over which of us belonged to the better sex. For the most part they consisted of her saying "Girls are better than boys," and my saying "Boys are better than girls," but sometimes they could get pretty legalistic. Sometimes, for instance, we would have competitions to see who could get dressed faster—for some reason this was an important issue—and if I won, she would say that it was no fair because boys were slobs who didn't care how their clothes looked whereas girls had to be more careful about neatness; and if she won, I would say that it was no fair because boys had to put on more clothes than girls—socks being, for some reason which come to think of it still eludes me, *de rigueur* for boys but not for girls. We used to have heated debates over socks.

Then, around the age of nine or so, I got tired of that argument. It started to seem silly. Someone had told me that the difference between males and females was that men had more quick energy and strength while women had more staying power. That meant, he said, that if you wanted someone to change a flat tire—or, for that matter, to toss it around for a while—you wanted a man, but if you wanted someone to carry it ten miles to the nearest gas station, you wanted a woman. That seemed fair to me. Tossing a tire around sounded like a better deal than trudging along with it for hours. (Later on, when I learned that women usually lived longer, I was to translate this trade-off into a deal whereby I got to roister around all I wanted in my youth in return for losing a few years of my tenure in the nursing home. It still seemed like a good deal.)

Anyway, I began to perceive that the whole argument was, in this case quite literally, childish. I mean, who cared who got dressed faster? One by one, the carefully worked-out arguments and counterarguments for the superiority of one sex or the other were put away, by my sister and myself, along with other toys of childhood.

Obviously, we were premature. We should have kept at those arguments, because they were ahead of their time. This became clear to me a number of years ago while listening to a television sports announcer explain why women tennis players should get just as much tournament money as men tennis players. The argument was that the women were almost as good as the men—hadn't the world's best woman player recently defeated a fifty-five-year-old has-been on nationwide television?—and, more important, professional tennis was an entertainment, not a sport, which meant that the players should be rewarded according to their draw at the gate rather than their skill.

That kind of suddenly uncovered distinction ("Girls are *neater* than boys") was exactly the kind of special pleading that distinguished the boys-versus-girls debates of my childhood. It is back with us again. The difference is that this time the boys are keeping quiet.

It's entirely possible, for instance, that you've heard the entertainment-not-sport argument, according to which women tennis stars do in fact get paid as well as the men, though almost no one pretends that the best, or twentieth-best, woman professional would have much of a chance against the best man. It is most unlikely that you've heard anyone carry that argument to its logical conclusion: that purses be awarded according to popularity rather than success on the court (alas for John McEnroe). Or worse yet: that since men's athletic events, especially football, are vastly more popular than the female equivalents, shouldn't all those Title IX crash sports programs for college women be turned back?

You haven't heard that kind of if-*x*-then-*y* back talk from men, because many of them have a certain amount of residual chivalry when it comes to arguing with ladies, and because many of the others consider the whole idea of such arguments childish, which it is. As a result, there is by now virtually no similarity or difference between men and women, whether seen as conditioned or innate, whether real or imagined, which has not been discovered to be evidence that girls are better than boys. A childish exercise, all right—but then, legislators tend to be childish, as do, God knows, the media, as do many of the people around us. I am writing this shortly after the Supreme Court has in effect declared that men are okay for cannon fodder but women aren't. So the childishness can get serious, even murderous. At which point it becomes necessary for men, in their own interests, to stop playing grown-up and listen to what's being said. Also to answer back.

In addition to chivalry and self-respect, one other reason that men have largely held back from the Augean prospect of genuine feminist debate is a shrewd premonition of futility: Who could make sense of *that?* Who can hope to argue with Susan Brownmiller or Adrienne Rich? (Might as well argue with a spastic colon.) Who can hope to wrestle with the tangle of conflicting propositions that result when all feminist statements are put together? (Might as well wrestle with a snakepit.)

Recording his first impressions of Senator Joseph McCarthy in *Senator Joe McCarthy,* Richard Rovere distinguished between the more familiar "big lie" and McCarthy's new technique of the "multiple untruth," and in the process foresaw the difficulty faced by anyone trying to grapple with contemporary feminist polemicists:

The "multiple untruth" need not be a particularly large untruth but can instead be a long series of loosely related untruths, or a single untruth with many facets. In either case, the whole is composed of so many parts that anyone wishing to set the record straight will discover that it is utterly impossible to keep all the elements of the falsehood in mind at the same time. Anyone making the attempt may seize upon a few selected statements and show them to be false, but doing this may leave the impression that only the statements selected are false and the rest are true.

The only way to hope to make any sense of the whole program is to work from the specific to the general—to begin with particular feminist assertions and keep careful track of the stages by which they dilate into feminist theory, keeping especially watchful for fudgery and flip-flops.

Take one example, pretty much at random, of a difference between men and women that at first glance might not seem to be ideological grist: the statistical fact that about three times as many American men as women commit suicide, while about three times as many American women as men attempt suicide. What are feminists likely to make of that?

Well, to begin with, we might ask what conclusions could be expected to come out of an evenhanded discussion, so as to contrast it with what in fact has emerged. In the following exchange, "M" is the male speaker, "F" the female.

M: Obviously, women are nine times as incompetent as men.

F: Obviously, women try and fail to kill themselves more often than men because despite their grief they feel, as women, a wish to nurture and preserve life, even their own.

M: Women are more prone than men to use half-serious or fake suicide attempts as "cries for help" to get attention. This is because, compared to men, they are self-pitying, self-indulgent creatures who are unscrupulous about using emotional blackmail.

F: If women are that way, it's only because they have been patriarchally conditioned to depend excessively on the support of others—the "Cinderella complex."

M: Women try to kill themselves more often than men because they are weaker—less equipped to stand the pressures of modern life.

F: Men do kill themselves more often because they are weaker —they die sooner, contract more diseases, are more likely to be alcoholics, drug addicts, criminals, and so on. The suicide rate is just one indication of how they are less adapted to living in the world.

M: If men are that way, it's only because they have been matriarchally conditioned to be good little soldiers—they have been raised in the military tradition that their own lives are expendable when socially inconvenient.

F: If women have left it to men to do all the killing and dying, it's only because they've been raised in the tradition that they themselves are the vessels of posterity, to be protected at all cost.

M: Men kill themselves more often than do women because life is harder for them.

F: No, women try to kill themselves more often because life is harder for them.

M: Men kill themselves more often because they are active creatures, more inclined to take matters into their own hands; whereas women are passive, more inclined to let things happen.

F: That famous male decisiveness is really just a kind of neurotic absolutism: Men are drawn to death because of its finality; whereas women, less given to black-and-white abstractions, hold back from anything so brutally conclusive.

M: Men are braver.

F: Women are smarter.

Or, finally, distributing these positions ideologically and summing them all up:

M: Men commit suicide more often than women, and attempt it unsuccessfully less often, because their lives are harder; their standards higher; the casualties in their ranks greater; their fondness for frivolous, morbid fantasies less pronounced; their willingness to impose on others much lower; and because when they decide to do something, they are less inclined to go about it in a half-assed way, or to botch it.

F: Women try to kill themselves more often, and succeed less often, because while their lives are harder, at the same time their attachment to life is greater, since they can usually avoid the pathological male tendency to live it by abstract either-or standards. That fewer women go through with suicide proves, not that they have things softer, but, on the contrary, that they have been hardened to endure more suffering—as indicated by all the women who attempt suicide. When a woman does kill herself (Marilyn Monroe, Sylvia Plath), it is because even she can't bear things that would have broken a man long before. These things are the fault of men (Hollywood producers, Ted Hughes). When a man commits suicide (Ernest Hemingway, Yukio Mishima), chances are it's just a final acknowledgment of his own spiritual bankruptcy.

It has been a good long while since we've seen anything in print like M, above. A strange fact, that, when you consider how much has recently been written and said against such ideas, on the premise that they are, somewhere, all around us. F, on the other hand, ought to sound pretty familiar, at least in parts. Even if you haven't read Rich, Brownmiller, Dworkin, et al.—and it's not something I'm suggesting, mind you—it should ring some bells. It is the received orthodoxy of the day, influencing the determination of every issue, and you no more need to be directly familiar with its formulators than a medieval communicant needed to know Latin.

Just suppose, however, that one of the people going around saying things like that was taken out of the soothing echo chamber to which she had become accustomed and asked to account for her statements in a less hospitable forum—one such as exists between the covers of this here book, for instance. Suppose she were asked to explain such questions as how she expects to get away with saying that women are less decisive than men because they've been brainwashed to be that way and then saying that women are less violent than men because that's just the way they are; and suppose even further that she felt obliged to reconcile, or at least explain, such discrepancies.

It won't happen, of course, not in real life, where these people as a rule keep to themselves and won't stand for much back talk. But art is more tractable than life, and I propose to conjure a facsimile—determined as scrupulously as possible by what I've heard and read of feminist argument—of what such a person might say in such a position. So here is Mira, back from the previous chapter, doing her damnedest to make the whole thing make sense.

AUTHOR: What about all this talk, Mira, of how much gentler women are than men—more nurturant, less violent, and so on? A lot of your sisters go on as if this quality were a natural development of being born with a womb. And of course they've got lots of company in that opinion, down through history. Many others have felt that a special capacity for maternal feeling radiated outward from the womb, but then they also—the Greeks, for instance—thought that hysteria did, too. What I want to know is, which is natural and which isn't? Or is it both? Or neither?

MIRA: Neither. You don't have to think about that kind of idea very long to realize that calling sexual differences like that "innate" is just a short slide away from George Gilder-land, where woman's place is in the home, barefoot and pregnant.

AUTHOR: Actually, I want to see how you get out of saying that.

MIRA: Easy. There are at least two related ways of explaining the difference. First, ever since men figured out that they needed women to produce replicas of their darling selves, they've made it a point to sequester them away in little oubliettes, where other men can't get at them. Out of sight, out of mind—and also, unavoidably, out of combat.

Second, men haven't wanted women to fight because they don't want them getting anything on their own. They like everything to come from themselves, in return for submission, especially sexual submission.

AUTHOR: So all that Eternal Female business was so much male brainwashing. As my friend Neil puts it, "The only damn thing that made them worthwhile was their femininity, and now they say they got that from *us*." And a lot of you, to give you credit, have worked overtime to prove it, making a point of being as piggy as your worst ideas of what men are like. Some progress. As far as I can see, the major contribution of feminist consciousness-raising has been to give one-half of humanity a pretext for being less humane and feeling virtuous about it.

MIRA: Yes, that seems to be exactly as far as you can see. Your friend Neil at least is partly right. We do reject "femininity," by which he means, no doubt, a lot of tittering and simpering and submissiveness. We yield it to the drag queens—men invented it, and they're still better at it. We finally know exactly why men think it's the "special" part of us—because it's the part they made.

AUTHOR: Never mind the tittering and simpering. What about that maternal sympathy I was talking about?

MIRA: Part of the package. All that earth-mother crap about how women were put here to comfort and protect their little men, no matter how old they are; how if a woman ever feels like doing something for *herself,* she must be crazy.

AUTHOR: Right, then: We've established that femininity, with its cult of passivity and prettiness and earth-mother nurturers, is a male fabrication. Now, would it be too much to ask you to tell me what women *are,* then, if they're not—whatever you say they're not?

MIRA: Would you repeat the question? *(Giggles in gallery)* I'm afraid *(simper)* it was too much for my fluffy little head to handle.

AUTHOR *(keeping temper):* I'm trying to define a few terms here, and you people have a way of making that awfully hard. It's very difficult for me to know what to call that fifty-one percent of humanity to which you belong when you and your gang are just waiting to tell me, whatever term I use, that it's a patriarchal imposition. "Woman" and "female" are obviously out, being derived from male originals. Anything with only one syllable is automatically insulting to you. Would you prefer "Vagino-Americans"?

MIRA: You stole that cheap chauvinist gag from the *National Lampoon (boos and catcalls; fists and fingers),* which says a lot about you right there. "Woman" will do, for the time being.

AUTHOR: Good. Now what can we call that part of woman, if it exists, which hasn't been made in the "feminine" mold by the patriarchs? Or is there such a thing? Is there anything in female nature that is not the work of men? Or are you all just so many little golems, made over in our diminished image and sometimes getting out of control?

MIRA: No, no, no—if anything, the reverse: *Men* are the ones who behave like zombies, spinning out their abstract life-denying systems. It's women who have kept whatever contact our race has managed to hold on to with the basic facts of life. As Adrienne Rich, a more eloquent woman than myself, has written, "Female biology—the diffuse, intense sensuality radiating out from clitoris, breasts, uterus, vagina;

85

the lunar cycles of menstruation; the gestation and fruition of life which can take place in the female body"—*that* must be the saving remnant of our link with life, what's left over after man's war against woman and the living part of himself: "What is astonishing, what can give us enormous hope and belief in a future in which the lives of women and children shall be mended and rewoven by women's hands, is all that we have managed to salvage, of ourselves, for our children, even within the destructiveness of the institution: the tenderness, the passion, the trust in our instincts, the evocation of a courage we did not know we owned, the detailed apprehension of another human existence, the full realization of the cost and precariousness of life."

Or, in the words of another of our poets, Robin Morgan, our bodies are "aware of the locked-in relationship between humans and the biosphere—the earth, the tides, the atmosphere, the moon." That is why we can hope to prevail and endure, against all you have done and will do to us, because we are closer to life and unafraid of it—"undaunted by blood we who hemorrhage every twenty-eight days." *(Wild applause from gallery. Standing ovation. Spontaneous round of contrapuntal singing of "I Am Woman" and "Ride of the Valkyries.")* There remains that, and that is what men, out of fear or envy, have tried to obliterate by imposing their own weaknesses on us, in the form of "femininity."

AUTHOR: And again, what will we call this remnant, unsullied by patriarchal force? If male-determined femaleness is femininity, what is female-preserved femaleness?

MIRA: Well, aren't we the little Aristotle. Why are you men all so wild to *brand* everything with a label? If you insist on a name, call it "womanhood."

AUTHOR: Thank you. Now, can you tell me some of the distinguishing features of womanhood, as opposed to femininity? We've already established that maleness is characterized by brutality. At least I think we have. You wouldn't say, would you, that men are made brutal by female influence?

MIRA: Come on.

AUTHOR: Right. We're just made brutal. Evolutionary, no doubt. That is one of our major distinguishing features, along with—oh, let's see *(flipping through books on feminist bookshelf)* . . . necrophilia, egomania, of course fascism, Nazism and child molesting, perversion in general, obsessive goal-directed sexuality . . .

(Muttering from gallery: "Insensitivity, immaturity, crudeness, yuckiness, loudness, messiness, sweatiness, hairiness . . . ")

Right. And what are the corresponding female equivalents? What makes for womanhood? Since for men the list starts with brutality, for women it must be—un-brutality?

MIRA: Gentleness, in other words. Yes. Also caring. Also emotional depth. Endurance. Appreciation of the world, its beauty and fragility. Rachel Carson and Georgia O'Keeffe, for instance, are heroic sisters who held on to their womanhood in the age of Hemingway and Mailer. Sympathy, in all senses of the word: Women feel for others—

AUTHOR: I thought that was all "earth-mother crap."

MIRA: It is, when you men interpret it in your own narrow interests. That doesn't mean it isn't real on some level. Now let me continue. Women feel for others, they pick up more quickly on the moods and thoughts of others, they are more alert to the mutant shapes and shadows of the world around them, the plants and animals, the colors and stars and seasons. Where men are arid, women are copious; where men are goal-directed, women are field-oriented; where men abstract, women embody; where men reduce, women enrich; where men survey, women see; where men see, women feel; where men evacuate and lay waste, women absorb and burgeon; where men run frantically all over the map looking for something else to despoil, women remain, endure, and grow.

AUTHOR: In other words, as one of your sisters says, "Whatever she does," a woman "knows where to stop," because she doesn't go to the "mad extremes" of men.

MIRA: I don't recognize that. Who said it?

AUTHOR: Molly Bloom. Ha!

MIRA: Very funny.

AUTHOR: The century's foremost literary earth mother, and the creation of a man who thought an intellectual woman was a contradiction in terms. And it fits, and you know it fits, because the fact is that whatever you and your clan may call it, all this business about nurturing and burgeoning and being sensitive and insightful is the same old earth-mother number. As with all other ideas of womanhood, you like it fine so long as it doesn't get in the way of anything else you may feel like at some other time.

Like abortion, for instance. One of these days I would really like to hear how you self-promoted keepers of the flame of life can square that routine with your support of abortion on demand. Over and over again, your people have been saying that what sets men apart from women is their soul-killing dependence on lifeless abstractions; and yet here, on the major life-or-death question of our time, the issue of which turns on whether that being situated between conception and birth is to be considered as a human or as a thing, you invariably act as if anyone who feels any bond of humanity to it is a sentimental sot. And then you say that men are the ones who deny the reality of life, who turn away from it, who make everything abstract. Well, you just can't have it both ways.

MIRA: You just can't have it both ways. That really sums it all up for you, doesn't it?

AUTHOR: That's it. You got it.

MIRA: You just can't have it both ways. Wonderful. If you're a welfare mother or a rape or incest victim or a pregnant teen-ager, and you try to take a little control of your life and keep it from getting ruined—well, don't come crying to me about any children you may want to keep later, because you just can't have it both ways. If you feel like being both a mother and a person with some rights over her own body —well, tough, you just can't have it both ways. If you sometimes like to think that there may be something miraculous about your capacity to bear and bring forth life—well, fine, that makes you Molly Bloom. It may seem like a rough deal, but you can't have it both ways, and nothing is worse than contradiction.

That's the real difference between us, isn't it? Forget abortion and all that other stuff—what really outrages you is the thought that we're being logically messy, which is probably one of your definitions of "female." How typically male. Because one thing that women know in their blood—one thing never learned by the rarefied super-"rationalist" males who for so long have been forcing us into the brutal either-or "logic" of their "laws"—is that it just isn't possible to live a life without contradiction. Things aren't neat: That's the knowledge that your mothers have shielded you from. Life isn't logical. Sorry, but it's time you knew. Life isn't fair, either, in case you haven't noticed.

There would be something touchingly innocent about your demand that we can't have it both ways—in other words, can't ask for abortions when needed and also care for the children we do have; that a woman who submits her body to medical technology is thereby disqualified from expressing anxiety about what other technologies are doing to her or to the earth—if that kind of "logic" weren't so typical and malignant. As it is, monkish little sophists like you, with your kosher codes about mutually exclusive pigeonholes and your tribal taboos about one concept contaminating another concept, are in the process of "rationalizing" this inconsistent, messy, tragic but living world of ours, where the lucky ones have things both ways all the time and the unlucky ones don't get anything, into a place that no one of woman born would recognize or want to live in. The idea of a man—one of that half of the human race that has been allowed to have all the sex desired without ever worrying about getting pregnant—telling me that, when it comes to abortion, women can't have it both ways!

God, that's so typical. All that self-satisfied, oh-so-neat cutting up of life into something you can "deal with rationally." One thing I've learned from talking to men like you is what my sisters have been writing for years—that "logic" is just another phallic extension, like knives and bullets. You can see it in the way you all instinctively home in, like guided missiles—or what you men so revealingly call the "smart" bombs of the Pentagon, or like flies to shit—on one little point singled out from everything around it and immediately start worrying it and taking it apart, pontificating about how, if x is so, then y can't be so, and if y *isn't* so, then *z* follows. . . . congratulating one another for being "on target," for hitting the "nail on the head," for being "rigorous" instead of fuzzy or soft. God, it's so amazing the way your language gives you guys away—little boys always in the schoolyard with your eternal peter-meters, endlessly competing over which of you is best at turning himself into a tool.

Tools. Logical tools. Research tools. Tools of the trade. *That's* the difference between men and women, so obligingly demonstrated by yourself: the way you men make a virtue of totemizing, fetishizing everything, including parts of yourselves.

Tools. Man is a toolmaking animal. *Man* is a toolmaking animal. I learned that in elementary school, and it's a sentence that comes back to me every time I meet an intellectual who uses his wit as a prick, or a jock doing his best to turn his body to stone. Tools. Scalpels, guns, bats, cocks, forceps, stirrups, chastity belts, whips and chains . . .

AUTHOR: Let's get something straight here—

MIRA: My God, would you *listen* to yourself?

AUTHOR: Sorry. But I would like to have something—let's say "settled" between us. I would like to know where you think this—I borrow the word from your fellow feminists, and look forward to the day when I can give it back for good—phallocentric way of thinking comes from. I want to know its nature.

MIRA: Its nature. Its "essence." Exactly. You, tool that you are, want to boil it down and put it in a nutshell and shove it into one of five or six pigeonholes.

AUTHOR: Mixed metaphor. Sorry, couldn't help myself.

MIRA: Jesus Christ, you really are Exhibit A, you know that? I will repeat your question. You wish to know what is the "nature" or essence of this foul, cancerous, garbagey death machine. We're being raped and you want to sit up there splitting the hairs on the rapist's head. Very well. Here is my answer.

Number one, I don't know for sure. That is one thing we have in common. I will opine, as they say, that it probably has something to do with the following facts. Men are genitally equipped with exposed, vulnerable, unretractable little appurtenances and women aren't. As a result, sexually men can think of themselves as externalized and dis-embodied in a way that women can't. That's number one. Men are physically stronger in the upper body region—that's number two. Men don't get pregnant—number three.

Finally, a million years ago, men, being simpleminded creatures, put these facts together and concluded that this externality, this ability to function in a way as *tools* of themselves, must be what raised them above those menstruating, parturiating females who were so ignominiously bound down to the earth by blood and biology. As a result, they immediately fell in love with their own cocks, or, to be more accurate, with that way of thinking of their own flesh and blood as something inhuman and detachable, which was to come into its own in the machine age, and later the nuclear age. They schooled themselves to think of parts of their own bodies as machines, therefore dead, and whipped themselves into imitating it. So they became half-dead themselves, and worshipers of death.

The first tool wasn't the wheel or lever—it was the cock. As Susan Brownmiller has pointed out, it was a tool like the club or arrowhead—a weapon, especially useful for reminding women of their place, which was underneath. It was the first tool, and its first political act was rape; and the patriarchal logic, language, and laws that we live under are all its offspring, its extensions, its bloody little bastards.

AUTHOR: Thank you for that interesting lesson in the origin of the species. I take it, then, that it would be safe to say that, in common with virtually all your political opponents, you believe that anatomy is destiny. You are a—how should we say?—biological determinist.

MIRA: There you go again with your labels. More tools, in other words. Obviously you haven't listened to a word I've been saying, or, for that matter, read those other radical feminists as carefully as you'd like me to think. Because one of the things we have said over and over is that we want to put an end to labels like that and the either-or mind-set they come out of. When we call ourselves "radical feminists," we mean *radical.* We're not just talking about getting a few raises and passing a few laws. We reject, we want *radically* changed, the mentality from which the laws and the economy and everything else spring.

Number one on the list of what we reject is patriarchal language and what goes with it: the way you men need to turn absolutely everything into *objects,* neat little signed-and-sealed categories like "cunt" and "ball-breaker," and, just now, "biological determinist."

This way of *nailing* down anything that moves, whether it be a woman or an insight, of *fetishizing* the universe of both life and the mind—*that's* what some of my sisters mean when they talk about men as lovers of death and bringers of death. Listen again—it might do you some good—to Robin Morgan in *Going Too Far:*

> I've changed too much for those games, and I'm in this process for good. I've learned that the "either/or" dichotomy is inherently, classically patriarchal. It is that puerile insistence on compartmentalization (art *versus* science, intelligence *versus* passion, etc.) that I abhor. We needn't settle for such impoverished choices. Reason without emotion is fascistic, emotion without reason sentimental (cheap feeling which is, in turn, fertile ground for the fascistic). Science and art budded from the same stem—the alchemist poets, the Wiccean herbalists, the Minoan and Druidic astrologer-mystics and mathematician-musicians.

And Adrienne Rich in *Of Woman Born:*

> I am convinced that "there are ways of thinking that we don't yet know about." I take those words to mean that many women are *even now* thinking in ways which traditional intellection denies, decries, or is unable to grasp. Thinking is an active, fluid, expanding process; intellection, "knowing," are recapitulations of past processes. In arguing that we have by no means yet explored or understood our biological grounding, the miracle and paradox

of the female body and its spiritual and political mean-
ings, I am really asking whether women cannot begin, at
last, to think *through the body,* to connect what has been
so cruelly disorganized—our great mental capacities,
hardly used; our highly developed tactile sense; our genius for close observation; our complicated, pain-endur-
ing, multipleasured physicality.

There is an inexorable connection between every aspect
of a woman's being and every other; the scholar reading
denies at her peril the blood on the tampon. . . .

And, for good measure, Mary Daly in *Gyn/Ecology:*

"The way back to reality is to destroy our perceptions of
it," said Bergson. Yes, but these deceptive perceptions
were/are implanted through language—the all-pervasive
language of myth, conveyed overtly and subliminally
through religion, "great art," literature, the dogmas of
professionalism, the media, grammar.

In order to overcome this inherited vocabulary of idi-
otology, Hags/Harpies must use our Double Axes to
hack away its false dichotomies. . . .

Now do you understand?

AUTHOR: Of course. You are romantics, of a particularly anti-
rational and, I might say, passé kind. You are the offspring
of the 1960s drug culture, of the McLuhan cult and transcendental this and that and psychedelic synesthesia and revolution for the hell of it—all that pimply rodomontade about
bursting the bounds of the senses, of society, of linearity and
syntax. "Blowing your mind," we used to call it, not guess-
ing how literally the slogan was to be taken by some people,
now battening on the genial doctrine that thinking is an
establishment snare and consequently, it is dawning on us,
making themselves, as an act of virtue, unfit for writing,
thinking, talking in sentences, or much of anything else
except for parroting people like your friends, watching television, and smoking grass, a basically boring drug whose

vogue is due mainly to the fact that it can make television interesting.

MIRA: Whew! Aren't we the last of the red-hot something-or-others! So you're saying—giving things your favorite, the nutshell, approach now—that radical feminism is a result of the decline of College Board scores and, incidentally, the West.

AUTHOR: Something like that. Erica Jong gave her book the wrong title. It should have been called *Fear of Thinking.* There is a kind of stupidity chic, never far from the surface in this country, for which you people have a disturbing affinity. Not that you're all stupid—many of you are far from it—but as you just demonstrated, smart or stupid, you find it hard to resist this "thinking through the body" drivel.

You're determined to hold on to that ace in the hole: that if an argument isn't working out the way you'd like, it must be because the language it's being conducted in and the laws of logic it's supposed to follow are patriarchal inventions, rigged against you from the start—as if some primordial chauvinist Jehovah just dreamed up the tendency for two apples added to two other apples to make four apples instead of three or five, or arbitrarily proclaimed that the angles of a triangle shall equal one hundred and eighty degrees, no more and no less, and that no entity shall be allowed to be both itself and not-itself at the same time, and all you have to do is topple his temple for the universe to rearrange itself in accordance with your blood-consciousness.

MIRA: The laws of math and geometry are not patriarchal inventions. The idea that those laws can be used as the standard of all human experience is. It's only on the blackboard, professorial descendant of the Mosaic tablets, that something can't be, as you put it, both itself and not-itself. In human life, that happens all the time. It happens especially at moments of intensity—those experiences of being simultaneously oneself and outside of oneself—of which orgasm is the most obvious, and to you probably the only real, example. What such experiences remind us of is that there are possibilities for freedom and meaning beyond what has been bequeathed us by the old words, the old

codes of exclusion. Sensing this, we're naturally drawn to
the inclusive, the suggestive, rather than to the hard-and-fast
—to poetry and parable instead of axioms and pronun-
ciamentos.

AUTHOR: *Against Our Will, Sexual Politics,* the kinds of slogans
we've been hearing from you all over the last twelve years
—is that your idea of poetry and parable?

MIRA: It's still a man's world, and you still have to talk like a
man sometimes to get attention. But listen to what we're
talking *about,* and you'll find most of us want something
beyond the old either-or terminology. That's why we're so
concerned with our inherited language and what it does to
the way we think, however many jollies you chauvinist
horselaughers may get about person-holes and mail-persons
and even (har-dee-har) person-persons. We want a new language so that we can have some new rules that will have a
chance to stick. People who want a new language seem
barbaric to people who like the old one just fine. Too bad.

AUTHOR: Exactly. As I said, you're romantics, of a rather
crude order. And about your kind of romanticism there are
two important points you should be aware of.

Number one, it is, according to evidence of the kind that
you people normally consider overwhelming, the invention
of men—just another patriarchal myth.

Number two, it is very close—in fact, as far as I can see,
identical—to the traditional female sensibility that you say
you're trying to break away from. All that business about
"new ways of thinking" apart from "traditional intellection," of hacking away the old dichotomies with your double axes and *feeling,* with your "highly developed tactile
sense," the truth—it all amounts to woman's intuition, the
kind of otherworldly sensitivity supposedly reserved for
creatures sequestered from daily life, in their parlors and on
their pedestals.

MIRA: About number one: Congratulations on demonstrating
yet again that everything we say has to be in terms determined by men. You're beginning to understand one of our
problems.

About number two: There's a big difference between the

"romanticism" pawned off on us by male writers and what we're trying to liberate. Male romanticism is all about getting *back* to something lost, always female, which some men intuitively sense they've cut themselves off from. Women may be thinking of the same kind of ideal, but not as something we have to reach out of ourselves to get. We're there already.

What's needed now is the creation of a language and network of social codes with which, unmediated by that intuition-to-dogma transductor, the male mind, we can make our sense of ourselves clear to one another. Which, by the way, is what's going on around you right now. That male "romanticism" was not, as you call it, an "invention" imposed on women; it was a derivative leeched and filtered out of them, then sold back to them as the genuine article. Today, we're living in the dawn of the real thing. In fact, come to think of it, it was a woman, married to one of your precious male romantics, who was the first to figure out the real nature of male "creativity" and represent it in a parable that every man has heard of without, of course, understanding.

AUTHOR: I give up.

MIRA: *Frankenstein,* of course, written by the wife of that spoiled ethereal angel and (naturally) first-class prick in his dealings with women, Percy B. Shelley. Like most women writers, Mary Shelley was only writing about what she knew intimately: a man trying, with his ideas and tools, to create a living creature—doing with his mind what a woman does with her body—and the consequences. Which is monsters.

AUTHOR: Actually, you're getting the Mary Shelley and Hollywood versions mixed up; in the book, Frankenstein's monster isn't monstrous at all—

MIRA: Oh, do shut up with your lit-crit nit-pickings. I'm making my final statement for now. You'll get your last word, of course. This is, let's not forget, your book, in which I am a tolerated visitor—a fact, incidentally, that I consider wonderfully representative of the world outside this book. Readers should remember that fact every time you have me say something wrong and then jump on it.

Mira Redux: A Conversation and a Conclusion

AUTHOR: Actually, Mira, your *Frankenstein* theory is simply a truism of feminist literary criticism, and of feminist writing in general—which is full of man-as-mad-scientist images and your womb-envy theory of male psychology. In fact, as far as that goes, everything you've said is typical, though spoken with more flair than usual. I haven't created you— just recorded you. I might add that your attempt to blame some man for any mistakes you may make is, as you put it, wonderfully representative: That trick was recorded, too.

MIRA: Flattery will get you nowhere. Let me speak my piece and retire from the stage, leaving the summing-up to the male lead, as usual.

Ahem. As I said, we feminists ideally prefer to think and talk in parables rather than in the linear forms of male "logic." *Frankenstein* is an example. It is no accident that it was written by a woman. For a long time now, people have been able to see that it is a prophetic parable, predicting what happens when the "analytical", "rational," toolmaking faculty gets developed out of all human proportion. Hiroshima, that's what happens. They've come to see, too, that this development is the greatest danger facing the world.

The thing we women are *now* able to appreciate, over a century and a half after a woman wrote it, is that *Frankenstein* is above all about *men.* No *woman,* then or now, would see any point to messing around down in the laboratory concocting little Boris Karloffs. It isn't a *human* sickness that the story's about, it's a *male* sickness, as seen by a woman, who was also able to see where it would lead.

One reason for the rise of feminism, and the "shrillness" of some feminists that so discomfits donnish old dilettantes such as yourself, is that her scary story gets scarier each year. Also, we now know who the real Frankenstein is: It's you guys, with those deadly phallic toys and tools in which you take such infantile pride.

Twenty years ago, people like us were members of Women Strike for Peace and groups like that, trying to ban the bomb. The bomb's still around, and now, having learned a thing or two, we're concentrating on what it is in you people that made you make the bomb in the first place:

97

that insane, deadly delirium that you are not of the same flesh and blood as us, that you are not tied down to this poor wounded planet as much as we are, that you can tinker and exploit and screw and strip-mine and bomb everything in your way, then move on, to the moon or wherever it is you expect to start over when you're finally through with this place. We're trying to save ourselves and, incidentally, men as well. You are, after all, our children. I sometimes wonder if you'll ever forgive us for that. *(Exit Mira, with retinue.)*

Does Mira sound like a caricature? Read that feminist *Roots,* Marilyn French's *The Women's Room,* whose main character is her inspiration, remembering that it is by far the best-selling "woman's book" of the age, and see if you think the Mira of these pages is any less reasonable than her original. Then, if you have the time and stomach, read through the theoretical and polemical literature of which the *The Women's Room* is the most florid flower, so as to fully absorb what the book is saying. Read, for instance, Mary Daly on breast cancer: how the "sickening symbolic 'semen' [she means medicine] swallowed by DES mothers under doctor's orders" is part of the "gynecological crusade to shorten women's lives" by first giving them cancer and then operating on them for it. Then turn to this passage in *The Women's Room:*

"Totally dependent," Samantha went on. [Samantha is talking about her no-good husband, whose name, so help me, is Simp. Samantha versus Simp: The names say it all.] I mean on everything. If they work or not, if they drink or not, if they go on loving you or not. Like poor Oriane." [Oriane!]

"Oriane?"

"You know, they were really living great, and she'd moved all the way to the Bahamas with him, and then one day he decides he doesn't want to live with her anymore and he just takes off and leaves her with a rented house, two boats unpaid for, three kids, and no money in the checking account. You heard about that."

"Yes. It's because they don't care about their kids. They just don't care about them. So they're free. Women are victims. All the way through," Mira heard herself say.

"And now she has cancer."

"What?"

Sam shook her head. "She's going in for surgery next week. Breast cancer."

"Oh, my God."

"It just goes on and on. Last year the woman who lives two doors down from me tried to commit suicide. . . ."

And now try to comprehend and hold this extraordinary fact: that, yes, she really means it; breast cancer belongs on that list of male awfulness; it, too, is part of the masculinist gynocidal campaign against women. And lest you think that Oriane is likely to be cured in her hospital full of male doctors, flip back a couple of hundred pages, to perhaps the most revolting birthing scene in literature; and if you want to see where *that's* coming from, browse around in any number of feminist studies written from the premise that male gynecologists are just clones of Dr. Mengele.

Then, if you will, reflect on the irony of so much sexist hate literature being turned out by people who, as one of their major articles of faith, hold that pornography is harmful because it feeds one sex's paranoid fantasies about the other.

Then, if you are male, reflect further that, for the last several years, women all around you have been reading books like *The Women's Room* (three million copies sold so far), and on the effect that fact may have had.

Where have you met Mira before? Lots of places, probably. Where have you heard speeches like hers? Better to ask, Where haven't you? There used to be gentlemen's clubs and bars where you could get away from that sort of thing, didn't there? Mira and her crew have pretty much succeeded in closing them down, as enclaves of chauvinist privilege, haven't they? When you think about it, considering that the all-female gathering is a feminist fixture, that doesn't seem quite fair—but they did it, didn't they? How did they get away with that?

Probably because you let them. Let's assume that, if you're a male, you've tried. You want to understand, to sympathize. Of course you're all in favor of the ERA— in fact, polls show that its support among men has consistently surpassed that of women. (Talk's cheap, Mr. Bandwagon-rider!) You believe in day-care centers, sharing of housework and child-rearing, opening of opportunities for women, equal pay for equal work, the abolition of all laws based on gender stereotype, and a realignment of the conventions behind them. (Nice try, tokenist!) You can't remember when you last lit a woman's cigarette. You open doors for women if and only if—you've worked this out very carefully—you would do the same for a man in the same situation, and even then you feel uncomfortable about it. (My heart's breaking.)

You've finally gotten to the point where you can distinguish, with about eighty percent accuracy, the women who are going to be insulted if you don't address them as Ms. from the women who will be insulted if you do.

You watch your language with a self-consciousness unmatched since you got stuck in the first row of Miss Pruitt's fifth-grade class, and periodically get yourself into the ghastliest syntactic tangles because of that impossibly awkward "he or she" formula. (Pedantic patriarchal elitist.)

You're turned off by much pornography, if not all of it (Ha!), but have your doubts as to whether it represents a clear and present danger sufficient to justify rewriting the Bill of Rights (First Amendment fetishist!).

As for sex (Ha! again)—well, as they say in the soaps, you've tried, God knows you've tried.

And the fruit of your efforts is that you find yourself the subject of a running symposium on the question of whether you are an unredeemable degenerate or merely a redeemable one.

Obviously you've missed the point somewhere. Listen to Mira. It isn't legislative turpitude you're being accused of. It isn't something you can *do* something about: How like a man to think that everything is simply a matter of *do*ing and un*do*ing! You want to know what it is? I will tell you, in two words.

Everything bad.

Just remember that, and the twists and turns of the representative debate recorded above will suddenly fall into a pattern. So will Mira's thoroughly typical resistance to any effort to make them make sense—that recoil from definition, that empurpled flood of antilanguage language and antilogic Luddism which, always there as a last resort, explains why you can never win an argument with her or her clan, ever.

Argument, did I say? When Mira hears the word, she reaches for the quotation marks. "Argument." "Reason." Male "logic." Patriarchal "definitions." Masculinist establishment so-called "scholars." "His"tory. All these, and the patterns they have imperfectly stenciled into her mind, have to be washed out with heart's blood. Above all, the fundamental rule of rational discourse, that you cannot take two opposite positions at the same time, has to be erased.

That is why these people are such easy butts for jokes, and why "humor" is another word given the quotation-mark treatment in their texts: because humor delights in exposing the incongruous, and incongruity is at the center of what they preach. They loathe consistency, as a patriarchal invention. It evokes visions of Doric entabla-

tures surmounted by effigies of Applonian male principles using their compasses and straightedges to rule the
female principle out of the picture, push the Erinyes back
underground. That is why, for instance, literary mad-
women are such a hot item these days, in contrast to Jane
Austen, say, who has a thing or two to teach these people
about the perils of willfully refusing to think things
through. (Kate Millett, as an example, has one sentence
on Austen, twelve pages on the Brontës.) Logic, consistency, "traditional intellection"—that is the proclaimed
enemy. The contradictions afflicting contemporary feminist theory are, as that old chauvinist Aristotle would
have said, essentials, not accidentals. Before all the other
rights demanded comes the right not to make sense.

Take, for instance, Mira on abortion. Look back and
you'll see that she never did sort it out—only protested
loudly against trying to sort it out. Fifteen years ago, Paul
Goodman remarked that rock stars singing against the
corporate power structure would be more credible if
they were not literally plugged into it through the cords
of their electric guitars; it was a useful remonstrance, just
as applicable today to the air-conditioned primitivism of
any group carrying on alternately about man's hubristic
manipulation of life and his superstitious scruples about
aborting it. Whatever else is going on here, it's clear that
rule number one, that you can't have it both ways, hasn't
been invited. It never is.

That is why, to take another example, the same people
who protest that pornography dehumanizes women by
representing them as disembodied genitalia can line up
for Judy Chicago's *Dinner Party,* where they will see a
triangular table set with rows of stylized vaginas on dinner plates, each framed, as if stuffed and mounted, by a
place setting complete with knife and fork. It should be
enough, you would think, to make Larry Flynt sick. But
here it is art because—and this is the nub, the pith, the

whole point, this is *it—male heterosexuals aren't involved.*

That is all ye know, and all ye need know. Forget about consistency, you silly boy. Just remember that one criterion. Understanding it would have solved everything for the poor confused bloke in this story from *The New York Times* of February 10, 1981:

One afternoon not long ago, a man trudged into the office of Women Against Pornography on Ninth Avenue.

"I'm glad I saw your sign," he said. "I need some help. Some people want to place homosexual statues in my park. I want to stop it." He was referring to a plan, which has stirred intense debate, to place a sculpture by George Segal of four homosexuals in Christopher Park.

Two women on duty in the office looked at him quizzically.

"We are for the statues," one of the women said. "I signed a petition *for* them."

There was a long moment of silence. "I thought you were women *against* pornography," the man blurted out.

"We are," the woman said. She explained, however, that they defined pornography as actions or materials that degraded women. The group, she said, is not opposed to homosexuality. In fact, she suggested, many feminists favor homosexuality as a normal, healthy sexual practice.

"What about degradation of the human race?" the man asked, and he stalked out.

Considering the strong streak of antigay sentiment in some feminist literature, it was disingenuous of that Women Against Pornography woman to say that "many feminists favor homosexuality as a normal, healthy sexual practice." It would have been closer to the truth if she had said, "We favor it when we figure it is in our interests to do so. By the same token, although we oppose pornography (sexually explicit representations of the human body that degrade women), we favor erotica (sexually explicit representations of the human body that do not degrade women). We can tell the two apart because, whereas the former turns some men on, the latter turns some of us on. And so *The Dinner Party* is admissible— is in fact cause for celebration—because of the proclaimed feminism of the artist; the liturgical atmospherics attending its presentation; the *Nihil Obstats* from the feminist press; the resolute high-seriousness of its female spectators in their determination not, whatever they do, to smirk, giggle, slaver, or puke; and the certainty that any stray male who does any of those things will forthwith be put in his place."

What all these amount to is labeling—and all the labels carry the same message: *For women.* That, and only that, is the test of feminist theory. In a utopian feminist state, tolerance of risqué material would be in precise inverse ratio to its tendency to activate the heterosexual male libido; and sexually frustrated men (and there would be a lot more of them, in a feminist utopia) would be reduced, like Fifties adolescents subscribing to nudist magazines or seeking out bare-breasted Maori tribeswomen in the *National Geographic,* to leafing through *Sexual Politics* and *Our Bodies, Our Selves,* unswathing the good bits from the pious cant, until the (doubtless female) librarian finally figured out what they were up to: "Did your mother give you permission to read this material? Go read your Willa Cather." If men like it, it's bad. That, and only that, is the principle at work—behind the pornography argument, the differing communiqués on homosexuality, and all the twists and turns, shuttlings and wafflings of Mira and the people for whom she speaks.

Which is to say that what we are dealing with here is not a philosophy, nor even an ideology; it is a party line, the sinuous tracing of the positions taken by an influential group determined to interpret every issue solely according to whatever best fits its interests at the moment, whatever absurdities, inconsistencies, or patent injustices that may lead them into. It was all spelled out candidly in the Statement of Principles of the New York Radical Women: "We take the woman's side in everything. We ask not if something is 'reformist,' 'radical,' 'revolutionary,' or 'moral.' We ask: is it good for women or bad for women?"

There it is: the Alexander's sword that alone can resolve the gordian knot of feminist dialectics. Try it on any issue you can think of, or on any of the movement's canonical literature. Let's take, for instance, that previously mentioned work, Kathleen Barry's (the title says it all) *Female Sexual Slavery*. Here is a representative passage:

> In Denmark pornography has had a definite effect on the attitudes toward sex crimes and accounts for a decrease in reporting of some sex crimes. The incidence of *reported* exhibitionism, peeping tomism, and physical indecency toward girls *decreased* over the ten-year period between 1960 and 1970. [Barry's italics]

That is, the decline in Danish sex crimes since the abolition of censorship just goes to prove the malignant effects of pornography. And what do you suppose an *increase* in those crimes would go to prove?

For the answer, turn to *Take Back the Night* (Laura Lederer, ed.), another antipornography tome, where the data on which Barry bases her conclusion is gerrymandered to produce the conclusion that certain sex crimes increased slightly. Thus proving, of course, the malignant effects of pornography. Confused? Don't be. Just remember: *"We take the woman's side in everything."* You will need to remember that, if you continue turning the pages of Barry's book until the end, where, having arrived at the place where one is customarily supposed to draw conclusions, the author faces the desperate tangle of contradictory propositions she has been piling up and, undaunted, womanfully soldiers through them:

Political change means confrontation with the values, institutions, and individuals which keep women colonized. Sex colonization assumes sex as an automatic right of men, but sexual intimacy precludes the proposition that sex is the *right* of anyone and asserts instead that it must be earned through trust and sharing. It follows then that *sex cannot be purchased, legally acquired, or seized by force* and that women must oppose all practices which promote "getting sex" on those bases. [Barry's italics]

So far, familiar enough: Sexual freedom is a patriarchal plot (that's what the second sentence means) and so there ought to be laws against it. Of course—it has been one of the book's main arguments—such laws that do exist, notably against prostitution, are all of them bad, because made by men. They are all either too lenient (thus in effect institutionalizing prostitution and degrading women) or too harsh (thus persecuting women who have been forced into their trades by patriarchal so forth and so forth).

That is the argument as it stands by the end of Barry's book: Legalizing prostitution degrades women; outlawing prostitution degrades women. An impasse, one might suppose.

One would be wrong. With that platitudinous perfect pitch which will astonish only those unfamiliar with the literature, Barry lights on just the right formula—one simple, impressive, trendy, latinate, much-in-the-newspapers, inoffensive, real-sounding, no-meaning, sweet little lullaby of a word: "Decriminalization [Ah!], which is the basis of the system of toleration [No, I didn't know that "toleration" was somebody's "system," either. No, she doesn't say whose], is the only means of taking women

out of the *official* status [her italics, again] of either criminal or prostitute." What "decriminalization" means, it
turns out (and I can hear Mira in the background now,
groaning over my macho insistence on defining everything) is that the state should legalize prostitution but
pretend not to, and in addition make regular, *sincere*
gestures of abhorrence, presumably by loosing armies of
feminist uplifters on their fallen sisters. (Never mind that
we've been that route before: It's called the Salvation
Army.)

Well, anyway, that's settled. And so, on the last page
of *Female Sexual Slavery,* as the book draws to a close, the
author ends up coming down once and for all on one side
of the issue: "Neither should we interfere with women
who enter prostitution freely, be they self-employed professional call girls or high-status African prostitutes, as
long as they can freely leave their work any time they
choose." But before you head for the aisles, read that
sentence again carefully. There is a word in there,
sounded twice, innocent enough at first but, to those
schooled in the idiom, loudly ticking away. The word is
"freely."

It becomes necessary at this point to realize that one of
the central principles of Ms. Barry and her school is that
the word "free," along with all its derivatives, is *always*
a male hoax. Remember: *"We take the woman's side in
everything."* Corollary: No woman who ever does something you would not like her to have done can be held
to have acted freely.

That is the corollary according to which women can,
for instance, see an offensive television commercial di-
rected at women, designed in strict accordance with polls
of women shoppers, on behalf of a product sold only to
women, and then get mad at men about it. It is the
assumption behind the fact that you, you poor male
shmuck, are supposed to feel guilty because their moth-

ers once wore fashionably uncomfortable clothes. And it is the principle that, halfway down the last page of the book, one sentence after she has apparently given a grudging endorsement to woman's right of sexual self-determination, enables Kathleen Barry to pull this little switcheroo: "And I assume that we must determine a woman's ability to freely enter or leave institutions of sex colonization based on her actual conditions and not simply on her perception of them or her desire to participate regardless of the conditions." That is, it doesn't matter whether our benighted young woman *thinks* she's well off, or even whether she cares. The matter is not in her hands, but to be determined by—"we." Guess what "we" are likely to think.

This is the real thing here, the authentic Orwellian voice—the FREEDOM IS SLAVERY chiseled above the entrance to the Ministry of Truth, the windings and double-bindings of the *Animal Farm* pig line. It is language in the service of the boot and fist, the piercing scream with eyes closed, hands on ears, face turning peony and seeming to twitch apart into separate zones. It is what you get when you allow books to be written by people whose logical and semantic range has all their lives been circumscribed by the dimensions of the placard, suitable for marching with, or by the length of the slogan, suitable for chanting. You get a collage of alternately indignant and pious mantras whose composite meaning, one is meant to understand, is in no way referable to logical or even syntactic connections—which are all traceable to the corrupted synapses of that patriarchal Trojan horse, the brain—but to an extratextual, metalogical body of faith.

Putting it less grandly, *Female Sexual Slavery* is willfully, proudly, triumphantly—and typically—stupid. Intellectually, it brandishes its stump in the reader's face. It makes a virtue of its author's inability to write a clear sentence or think her way out of a paper bag. These

become virtues when the test is purity of heart, and delib-
erateness would be a sign of "traditional intellection."

The civil impulse, in such instances, is to avert the eyes
in embarrassment, as at other public demonstrations of
infirmities—which is precisely why the people qualified
to judge these books have not been reviewing them. An
understandable reaction, but the consequence is that yet
another bit of humbug appears on the bookstands, pep-
pered with imprimaturs from Susan Brownmiller ("Exposes the dark side of sexuality and dares to ask the
crucial question . . . "), Gloria Steinem (" . . . exposes
and documents the international slave trade that is a
mockery of human right . . . "), Adrienne Rich ("This
powerful and compassionate book . . . "), and the *Los
Angeles Times* ("A powerful work filled with disbelief,
outrage, and documentation . . . "), planting in the minds
behind a million pairs of eyes that will never actually scan
the first page the impression that, somewhere, something
else beastly has been proven about men.

In a sad way, it's not Kathleen Barry's fault. In a sensi-
bly run commonwealth, it would have been made clear
to her years ago that she had no special gift for writing
or thinking and should seek fulfillment in other ways. In
almost any other field that calls for the putting of words
on paper, that would have been made clear. Among the
areas of study taken seriously by people who read, feminism stands almost alone in that its mandarins encourage
this kind of thing. That is why I have spent this much time
on Ms. Barry's poor pathetic barrel of fish: She is not a
lone geek on display; she is, in fact, representative, symptomatic.

As Mira likes to say, look around you. Take a close
look at some of these books and a close listen to what
their readers are saying. You will discover that Barry's
reflexive resistance to logical sequence and consistency is
not restricted to her book—it is a recurrent feature of

most any proclaimed feminist classic of the last fifteen years that you may bother to read. You will discover the recurring—and, to me, I must confess, tragic—fact that radical feminism at its primary level is hopelessly conflicted, and that consequently its distinguishing intellectual feature is a rebellion against reason, which it habitually stigmatizes as male in origin.

That is why, increasingly, these people seem to be talking only to one another; why even as their cause was apparently prospering, they were shrinking into ever tighter and smaller redoubts; and why their network of communication has come increasingly to resemble a herd of circus elephants in a ring, holding one another's tails —Adrienne Rich parroting Susan Brownmiller, Susan Brownmiller in raptures over Kathleen Barry, Kathleen Barry advancing the "positive paranoia" of Mary Daly, Mary Daly quoting page after page of Adrienne Rich. The idea keeps creeping past their outworks that what they are fighting is not the world of men but simply the world, where heading north means not heading south, where it is never noon and midnight at the same time, and where—oh, hateful words—you really can't have it both ways.

4

Mrs. Jellyby and the Montagu Doctrine

WHAT do you really think of *Sexual Politics?*" I once asked an ardent feminist who, being also a specialist in nineteenth- and twentieth-century literature, could not help noticing Kate Millett's relaxed way with the truth.

"As a work of criticism, I admit it's an embarrassment," she said, "but I think it was valuable as a polemic."

Fair enough—a polemic cleverly disguised as a doctoral dissertation and, later, critical study, with the scholarly apparatus serving the same function as a carnival barker's top hat; too bad Columbia University and *Time* magazine, suckered into making Millett, respectively, a doctor of philosophy and famous, weren't in on the joke.

Against Our Will? Another well-read feminist: "A crazy book in some ways, and its scholarship is [same word] an embarrassment, but you have to realize that that's how many of us really feel. It spoke for a lot of women." No doubt exactly the same was said on behalf of *Mein Kampf;* it's strange how this primal-scream rationale keeps coming from people who will then tell you that the screaming female is a male chauvinist myth.

THE **MYTH** OF THE **MONSTROUS MALE**

The same answer about *The Women's Room:* "That's how many women *feel.*" (A lot of women feel like paranoid lunatics, then.)

How about that *Ms.* favorite, Elizabeth Gould Davis's *The First Sex,* about which John Greenway, reviewing this book in the *National Review,* has written: "I have experience and some certification of authority in several scholarly fields through which Davis tramples in her hobnailed boots—anthropology, archaeology, mythology and linguistics—and I must say I have never before seen so much palpable nonsense gathered in one book"?

Here, let it be recorded gratefully, the feminists themselves have found it a bit fruity, even for them: The Redstockings have quite accurately characterized "the praise given to Elizabeth Gould Davis' *The First Sex*" as a symptom of "reactionary separatism." Two feminist writers, Amy Hackett and Sarah Pomeroy, pretty effectively exposed its scholarly fraudulence in an article in *Feminist Studies.* And even Adrienne Rich admits that it has been "an embarrassment to academic feminists intent on working within strictly traditional and orthodox definitions of what constitutes serious knowledge"—you know, like facts and logic. In other words, another embarrassment.

Speaking of Rich, what of her own *Of Woman Born,* and that other exemplary feminist work, Mary Daly's *Gyn/Ecology?* Well, let me remind you: Rich is the one who thinks that all males are child molesters, and Daly is the one who thinks male gynecologists are all gynocidal conspirators. Well, then, how about Andrea Dworkin, Robin Morgan, Kathleen Barry, Phyllis Chesler, Gloria Steinem? Come on. Take a good look. Embarrassments, one and all. How about *Take Back the Night,* an anthology of antipornography essays by thirty-two feminists? Look at the contributors: Kathleen Barry, Susan

Brownmiller, Phyllis Chesler, Andrea Dworkin, Robin
Morgan, Gloria Steinem, Adrienne Rich—in sum, the
same old flock of embarrassing turkeys.

Although, to be sure, several worthwhile historical
and autobiographical works have come out that, because
concerned with women, are loosely called "feminist,"
the fact remains that when it comes to theory or even
polemics, radical feminists—after well over a decade of
books, articles, speeches, and debates—have so far failed
to produce a single major work, endorsed by their own
reviewers, that is *not* an "embarrassment." The question
is, why is that? And the answer is that books are made of
paragraphs made of sentences made of words, all of them
related to one another by rules of logic, which these
people are against. They are against choices, which they
refer to as "either/or dichotomies."

Often, as I have said, they are able to get away with
it because the volume is up too high for anyone to pay
much attention to the message, and because the noise is
coming from so many different directions that coor-
dinating them seems out of the question. Over here,
the Women Against Pornography representative saying
that feminists support male homosexuals; over there,
Mary Daly and the Redstockings giving vent to some of
the nastiest antigay sentiments this side of Dade
County; over here, a host of women telling you that
their sex has failed to write as many great books and
invent as many great things as men have because of patriarchal conditioning; over there, yet another host telling you that women have failed to commit as many
atrocities as men because, actually, they're just naturally
nicer. Over here, words like "nurturant" and "life-
affirming"; over there, a steely-eyed, hard-mouthed
knot proclaiming anyone opposed to its program of
abortion-on-demand a sentimental slob. The list goes
on, indefinitely. Trying to grapple with it is like trying

to stop locusts with a rifle. No wonder most men have given up.

There is, however, one theoretical region in which most of these pronouncements sooner or later converge, and which can therefore be taken as a kind of philosophical touchstone for the whole: feminist history. Feminist polemists, not always finding reality similar to the way they say reality is, are often fond of appealing to history —the more remote and obscure, the better—as a kind of all-purpose verifier, the result being an unspeakable snarl of contradictory speculations that makes perfect political sense the moment you cease expecting it to make any other kind.

So let us spend some time trying to understand the philosophy of feminist history, in the hope that it may be a kind of skeleton key. Start by imagining a committee, convening regularly during the late Sixties and early Seventies, moving step by step according to the following impulses:

1. First of all, we have to watch out for cyclical or static theories of history. We are a progressive movement, so our theory of history must include the idea of progress: History must *go* somewhere.
2. However, if we accept the traditional yardsticks of progress —technological advances, widening enfranchisement, and so on—then we endorse the phallocentric civilization through which these developments have occurred, and we're asking for more of the same. We mustn't do that.
3. On the other hand, if we then agree that under the male onslaught of "progress" things have really been regressing from day one, our cause becomes hopeless. Mustn't do that either.

A problem. Let's diagram the possibilities.

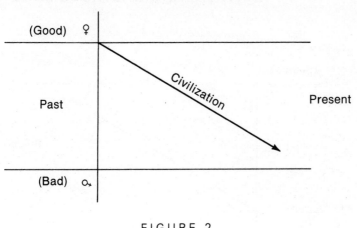

FIGURE 1

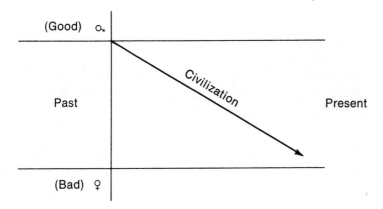

FIGURE 2

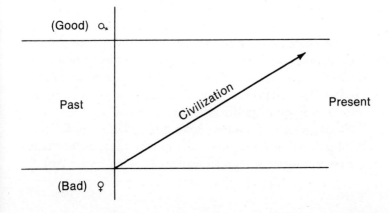

FIGURE 3

THE **MYTH** OF THE **MONSTROUS MALE**

FIGURE 4

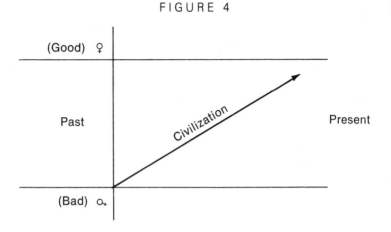

Figures 2 and 3 are included only for the sake of thoroughness. They are the enemy. Figure 2 outlines the once-fashionable idea that a culture's future depends on maintaining its virility—that Rome or Britain or what have you started declining and falling when female influence began to predominate, when they let themselves go effeminate and soft. Figure 3 is just the old story of Apollo and the Furies: Civilization is achieved insofar as the rational male principle rises above and represses the chaotic female primal matter. We know what to do with that kind of talk.

Okay. That leaves figures 1 and 4. Let's consider them side by side. Which to choose? Each presents difficulties.

Figure 1 shows that the more men have taken control of civilization, the worse they've made it. An absolutely crucial idea, but one that can lead to either despair or primitivism, *nostalgie de la boue,* racial recollections of the Golden Age: all powerful stuff, but all escapist, incompatible with hopeful political action.

Figure 4 says that things have gotten better as women have gained in influence—an inspiring idea, except that it's already been shown to lead to Woman as the Angel

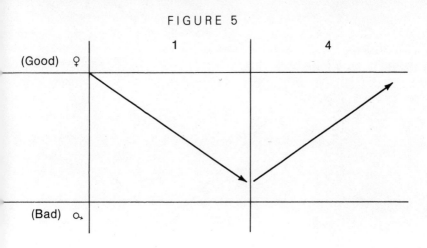

FIGURE 5

in the House, nature's noblest and finest product, evolved out of the crude, mucky earth where man is stuck: in other words, the Ruskinian pedestal from which we've finally succeeded in descending. Obviously, that won't do either.

It is at this moment that, I imagine, some unsung genius makes one of those simple, revolutionary recognitions that (literally, in this case) changes history. She realizes that there is still a patriarchal agent, so innocent-seeming that no one has noticed it, which has been subtly frustrating their efforts. It is that vertical line between the two figures. What is that line saying? "Choose one or the other." Either-or: the fundamental premise of masculinist logic! The enemy incarnate! Remove that line, think integratively rather than segregatively, and it all comes clear—*voilà*—the diagram of feminist history (see Figure 6).

To be sure, ideas of the exact location of coordinates *A* and *B* remain sketchy, to say the least. Kate Millett equates turning-point *B* with the mid-nineteenth-century/early-twentieth-century development of feminism, in relation to which the phallicist propaganda of

FIGURE 6

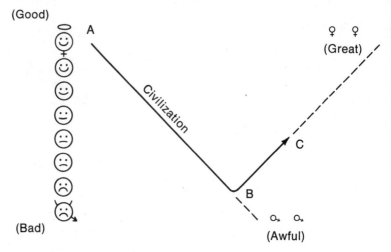

Lawrence, Miller, and Mailer constitutes one of those counterrevolutionary eddies that predictably vex any revolutionary tide. The members of Women Against Pornography maintain that the revolution-and-counter-revolution phenomenon has a later date: The modern woman's movement is the turning point, pornographic movies the inevitable reaction.

On the other extreme, Elizabeth Gould Davis and her school (of whom there used to be lots, including Gloria Steinem, although recently they show signs of dwindling) place *B* in the future. Note this from Davis's *The First Sex:*

In the new science of the twenty-first century, not physical force but spiritual force will lead the way. Mental and spiritual gifts will be more in demand than gifts of a physical nature. . . . And in this sphere woman will again predominate. She who was revered and worshiped by early man because of her power to see the unseen will once again be the pivot—not as sex but as divine woman—about whom the next civilization will, as of old, revolve.

As for *A,* the Fall, that occurred in prehistoric (hence, conveniently, unrecorded) times, when, discovering that women needed their help to get pregnant, men forcefully put an end to the golden age of the matriarchies— although here again the date is elusive: In one of the literature's truly dumbfounding footnotes (the talismanic virtue of footnotes to bestow scholarly authority is one of the movement's main superstitions), Robin Morgan amends the statement in the body of her text that "half the human species has been suffering for the past 5,000 years" as follows: "I have learned since that it has actually been ten to twelve thousand years since the rise of patriarchy." (Indeed.)

Those in the movement who go in for deep thinking have a theory that the Fall may have been not merely prehistoric but prehuman, cellular—the mutant y chromosome of the male sex screwing up the primordial oneness of the x's, then going on to spread its twisty way around the world and (now) solar system. . . . (Look, I *know* it sounds absolutely stark raving bonkers, but that happens to be the theory behind the fact that cancer metaphors come second only to Nazi metaphors in the rhetoric. Don't blame *me.)* In feminist autobiographies and autobiographical fiction—*The Women's Room* is again a model—*A* is the entrance into puberty and marriage, in other words into the world of men, and *B* is the company of women, where the heroine is able to rediscover herself.

So the (suspiciously familiar) pattern of fall and rise, death and resurrection, works itself out in diverse ways, often inconsistent in its details but always telling essentially the same story: womanhood in the remote past, when everything was pure and wonderful; womanhood in the remote future, when the world will be a garden once more; men in between. The reason for its appeal is clear. It is a latter-day variety of Pelagianism, the gnostic doctrine that humanity in its origins is naturally inclined to goodness, that sin is a foreign agent which can be purged altogether if identified—sin being, here, male influence.

The midway position assigned maleness means that its attributes are neither fundamental nor inevitable. Woman is both civilization's root and fragrant evolutionary bud, tipping the ends of the twigs; man is in the place of sin and capitalism in, respectively, Christian and Marxist history: a (perhaps) lamentably necessary but in any case certainly disagreeable intermediary stage in humanity's progress from the good times that were to the great times that will be.

It is not just the congruence with traditional Western millenarianism that accounts for the appeal of this pattern to so many feminists. It also fits the standard poetic treatment of woman as alpha and omega—preceding man as mother and succeeding him as widow; nursing, swaddling, embracing, and finally laying out the troublesome life that flares and gutters under her eyes: "The aged sisters draw us into life: we wail, batten, sport, clip, clasp, sunder, dwindle, die: over us dead they bend" (James Joyce's *Ulysses*). In a sense, feminist history is just the latest in a long line of myths to be evolved out of the observation that women usually live longer.

Perhaps the biggest reason for its popularity, however, is that it gives a theoretical basis to what, after much bafflement, I have finally discovered to be *the* feminist position on the essential question of nature versus nurture, the extent to which sex differences are inborn or conditioned. I am proud of this discovery. At first it seemed unattainable. For if there's anything we've learned not to expect from radical feminism, it's consistency (they are, remember, against it in principle), and in this particular question—considering that members of

the same movement can demand the liberation of mur-
deresses as social victims and the castration of rapists as
hopeless degenerates; that between the covers of one
book, *Of Woman Born,* Adrienne Rich can argue that all
fathers are child molesters by nature and then urge that
we sympathize with a mother who butchered her entire
family, because, after all, we don't know what social
pressures made her that way—the contradictions would
seem to be on the far side of derangement. Not so.
Feminist pronouncements on this fundamental issue plot
a mighty maze, but not without a plan. Here's how to
figure it out.

Draw three vertical lines down a sheet of paper, dividing it into four columns. In the column on the extreme
left, list five or so positive adjectives traditionally associated with maleness. In the second column, list five or
so negative adjectives traditionally associated with
femaleness. In the third column, list the same number of
negative "male" words; in the fourth, another list of
positive "female" adjectives. Different people will
choose different words, but your paper should come out
looking something like figure 7.

FIGURE 7

strong	weak	brutal	gentle
reliable	flighty	inflexible	reponsive
independent	dependent	selfish	supportive
adventuresome	timid	reckless	prudent
analytical	superstitious	legalistic	deep
M+	F−	M−	F+

Now, draw two brackets, one enclosing the first two lists,
the other the second two. Label the first bracket "Conditioned Differences," and label the second bracket "Innate Differences." And there you have the answer.

Thus, for instance, to help Mira in the previous chapter figure out just what she means by the difference between "femininity" and "womanhood," simply take any traditional female quality, find a positive word for it (F+), a negative word for it (F−), and situate them accordingly on the chart. Or take any fact of female life: In *The Women's Room,* for instance, motherly love is shown to come from the depths—

She felt something happening inside her body, a pull that started around her genitals, and pierced through her stomach, her chest, her heart, right into her throat. Her breast ached. She wanted to put it in his mouth; she wanted to hold him in her arms. . . . What she was feeling, she knew, was love, a love blinder and even more irrational than sexual love.

—while at the same time postpartum depression is the fault of the male-run hospital:

It never occurred to anyone to ask why women would kill the babies that had cost them so much pain, or kill themselves after the pain was over. But she had learned her lesson. They had the power. You had to act the way they expected you to act or they would keep the child of your own body and your own pain from you.

That is, if the mother nurses the baby, it's her doing; if she kills it, it's some doctor's.

Maybe you think figure 7 is a silly joke, insultingly elementary. Elementary it may be, but it is also the only way, so help me, to make coherent sense of what Mira was talking about, and what the many women of whom she is a type are talking about, when she and they alternate between, for instance, indignantly denouncing the "earth-mother crap" loaded on them by the patriarchy and then calling themselves "nurturant" and "life-supportive."

You cannot continue the four-part list very far without noticing that many of the permutations—for instance from "adventuresome" to "reckless" ($M+$ to $M-$) or from "timid" to "prudent" ($F-$ to $F+$)—are just positive or negative terms for the same thing, no more objectively distinguishable than the difference between "sweet" and "too sweet." That is why *language,* as opposed to anything real, is so important to these people. As with Judy Chicago's *Dinner Party,* they believe that the issue is not so much what is in the picture as it is the frame around the picture and the label put on the frame: A pornographic painting or literary passage becomes transfigured when labeled as part of a show for the edification of women, or included in a book on the sins of male authors.

The reverse applies equally. Take absolutely any page at all from the *oeuvre* of Andrea Dworkin, for instance, give it to a feminist literary critic as an example of the dialogue of some male novelist's female character, and it will not take her long to identify this character Dworkin as a fourth-rate Molly Bloom illustrating all the sexist stereotypes—the flow, the gush, the luridness and hysteria, the syntactic torpor and logical slobbishness and everywhere manifest all-around crappiness of mind. Then take away the *homo fecit,* and suddenly we have a leading feminist spokesperson, her excesses the mark of a noble soul hurt into anger, transcending male-imposed standards. So for all its fertile-Myrtle lyricism about woman as the source of everything living and everything real, modern feminism is often very close to the ultimate abstractness of total relativism: nothing true or false, good or bad, but thinking, and above all naming, makes it so. It accepts the substantiality of substance no more than it does the reasonableness of reason.

It may be observed that figure 7 is simply a logical outgrowth of the outline of history given in figure 6, the essential idea of which is that (to use the terminology of Mira's distinction) the "womanhood" originating in the state of nature (F+) degenerates into "femininity" (F−) when passing under the influence of maleness (M−). The corollary is that M+, such as it is, is a partially redeemed extract of M−, savage man socialized by woman halfway to humanity, at the cost of her own happiness and purity.

In other words, women are good for men and men are bad for women. (It is at this point that we are likely to hear of polls indicating that single women are happier than single men, and married men happier than married women, thereby showing that marriage is good for men but bad for women—a set of figures that, if accurate, would lead to the conclusion that the traditional female attitude toward marriage is a sign of the most virulent masochism, or stupidity, or both.) Again, this may sound like a ridiculously reductive version of a wide and still-evolving range of ideas. And again, I can only say, look around.

There are, certainly, exceptions, notably the Redstockings, who being Marxists have a taste for dialectic and a dislike for all ideas of inborn womanliness and what one of them, rebutting her sisters, has called "fantasies of lost matriarchies, female superiority and 'mother right.'" But the Redstockings are by their own testimony a fringe outfit, broadly repudiated by the movement because of their very desire to establish some sort of logical coherence.

Much more typical is, for instance, the most recent major exercise in feminist literary criticism, Marilyn *(The Women's Room)* French's *Shakespeare and the Division of Experience,* which simply applies the formula to the most seductive of cultural Rorschachs to produce the derivative formula that Shakespeare evolved from male values

126

to female values. "Shakespeare," said Keats, "lived a life of allegory"; the feminist Shakespeare is simply the latest in a series of allegories for the outline of feminist history, and for the central belief contained in that outline: that goodness is by rights an exclusively female possession; and that if men have anything good about them, they got it from women who were too generous or too pliant.

This idea has been around for a long time, but no one up to now has bothered to give it a name. I hereby suggest the Montagu Doctrine as an apt title, because it was anthropologist Ashley Montagu who crystallized the doctrine in one sentence. I will put it in italics: *"Most of their faults women owe to men, while men are indebted to women for most of their better qualities."*

There, in its simplest and most efficient form, is what those charts and graphs, and the statements from which they were derived, come down to. We should all be grateful to Professor Montagu for expressing it so pithily, and for including it in a book (much footnoted in *The First Sex,* by the way) that is so clearly, charmingly, gallantly, fustily Victorian. The truth, revealed for all to see in Montagu's *The Natural Superiority of Women,* is that to a remarkable extent the central premises of much feminist writing, when teased like snails out of their tough little shells, turn out to be reactionary.

Because of its impolitic failure to conceal that fact in the usual radical excelsior, *The Natural Superiority of Women* probably qualifies as yet another "embarrassment" on the feminist book list. But what it lacks in guile it makes up for in candor and a willingness to see through to the logical conclusions of its premises, that is lacking in any of its shelfmates.

Beginning with an epigraph from Matthew Arnold, Montagu uses phrenology, actuarial tables, and genetics (that twisted little *y* male chromosome again) to show

127

that women are gentler, more cultured, free from the "chronic state of sex irritation" that turns men into "a herd of prancing leering goats," free from the over-developed upper-body musculature that turns men into obsolete simian brutes, free from the hyperactive metabolism that makes men jumpy and burns them out at an early age.

He cites the familiar suicide statistics to show that men kill themselves in disproportionate numbers as an implicit acknowledgment of their relative unfitness for life, and that women pretend to kill themselves but hold back in the end because they are gentler and smarter. (See? I wasn't making that up.)

He congratulates woman for being, "by virtue of her natural reticences," "on the side of morality and the proprieties"; for being deep and nurturant; for devising the "positive accomplishment of considerable value" of swooning in times of stress instead of getting inefficiently tensed up like the macho male; for being closer to dem ole wellsprings of life; for being intuitive and avoiding the male's "uncanny faculty for separating his mind from his heart"; for having taken out only one-fiftieth as many patents as men have—thus saving the world a lot of grief; for not yielding to cerebral fads like abstract art (Georgia O'Keeffe and Grandma Moses are adduced—and so much for Helen Frankenthaler); for resisting those intellectual disciplines that strain the brain and lay waste the affective being (and so much for Hannah Arendt, too); for being "more in tune with the universe than men"; more concerned with personal relations and less with mechanical processes; and, in sum, for being "the creator and fosterer of life" while man is the "mechanizer and destroyer of life."

The catalog climaxes by evoking the Statue of Liberty: "Women are the cultural torchbearers in America; and even in the darkest parts of the land, wherever a gleam of light is seen it is usually cast from a source upheld by the hand of a woman."

First published in 1953, the book has proved to be a mother lode for virtually all the arguments that have recently been circulating, like air-conditioned air, through the Richian, Brownmillerian, Dworkinian, Frenchian, Barryan corridors—a prophecy in effect acknowledged by the 1973 issuance of a revised edition. With the exception of Elizabeth Gould Davis, they do not generally like to cite him—he is, after all, a man— but you can track the imprints of his facts and figures, and the conclusions he draws from them, in almost any prominent feminist polemic you are likely to consult. He believes that men are oversexed simians, that motherhood is the greatest thing in the world, that a woman's integrity depends on her ability to resist male influence: It is, in a prophetic nutshell, the argument of Millett, Rich, Dworkin, Brownmiller, Barry, French, *et al.,* years ahead of its time.

All of Women Against Pornography, for instance, lies implicit in the one sentence warning that television and comic books (which in 1953 meant "Howdy Doody" and *Batman*) are "murdering children's minds" and spreading (today the word would likely be "disseminating," with full weight placed on the underlying metaphor) a cult of violence.

What sets the Montagu book apart is that it does not then hesitate to draw the completely inevitable conclusion from its statements: that the superiority of women is directly connected to their separation from the world of machines, power, and money; that women trying to adopt male roles—and in Montagu's case, one automatically envisions suffragettes in bloomers—are deplorable mutants and traitors to their sex; and that woman's place is in the home, the real center of everything important.

The Montagu Doctrine is, of course, nothing but chivalric sexism—the old stereotypes with plus signs in front of them. It is naturally drawn toward the more tendentious theories of pop psychanthrosociobiology—naked apes, man-the-hunter metamorphosed into football teams and gun clubs, woman the grain-gatherer into the housewife in her kitchen, all that—and the doctrine of natural law that they support. Its message is that we are the way we are because that's how God, or some Darwinian surrogate, made us, period. Clearly, only the subtlest of shufflings is required to produce out of this the program of George Gilder, Jesse Helms, and their burgeoning horde, who really do mean it when they say that women are better than men, and that they aim to see to it that they stay that way.

The really troubling thing is that, at the same time, that is what so many feminists are saying, too. They consistently revert to the Montagu Doctrine, with all its nostalgic cant of mother right and the harmony of the hormones; just recall how much of what the ever-representative Mira had to say boils down to it, for instance. It may well be that we're in for another prolonged spell of this kind of milky drivel, led, as always in the past, by women, who will find themselves by degrees once again exalted (and thus, of course, degraded) right out of any active participation in the grungy business of public affairs. And it may come to pass that in another twenty or thirty years, some new Betty Friedan will therefore be required to spread the word that, you know, all that pedestal business really is a crock of shit, and so start the wheel rolling again.

If so, let it be remembered by that future generation of feminist chroniclers studying the collapse of their foremothers' cause that to a great extent the movement did it to itself—that when it came down to it, the old

Eternal Feminine proved to be the Eurydice from which too many of its members could not take their eyes, even to get her out from under.

And, of course, let it be also remembered that some men helped them do it to themselves.

Which brings us to the second Victorian figure of this chapter's title, Mrs. Jellyby. Mrs. Jellyby is the well-meaning lady in Dickens's *Bleak House* whose distinguishing eccentricity is that her charity to others is inversely proportional to their nearness to herself. For instance, she is forever donating the milk money of her own bedraggled children in order to buy alms for the orphans of Africa and Asia. She is, of course, a caricature of the Victorian clubwoman who is the direct forebear of today's feminist—but history is full of ironic loops, and today her incarnations are mostly men. The following, for example, is from Mr. Bruce Palmer (the one who in the same letter, quoted in an earlier chapter, tells me to read *Of Woman Born* and *Gyn/Ecology,* from which books his horror stories derive):

However, it has been woman's misfortune to suffer genital mutilation (Africa, the Middle East, the United States), foot binding (China), sacrificial burning (India, Europe, New England), unnecessary surgery, radiation, and medication, misogynist therapy built around notions of penis envy, gynocidal religions built around the idea of woman's responsibility for sin, her impurity, her inevitable pain, and less than equal economic and educational opportunities.

His message is a familiar one: that I, like males in general, ought to take upon myself the accumulated guilt for all atrocities committed against women in whatever distant climes and times—that the foot-bindings of dynastic China (traditionally carried out by women, incidentally) and the clitoridectomies of tribal Madagascar (traditionally carried out by women, incidentally) are evidence of my participation in the selective brutalization of women.

Meanwhile Mr. Palmer is, according to his letter, writing from Washington, D.C. Dare I suggest that if he wishes to gather evidence of sex-specific carnage, he should adjust what Dickens calls Mrs. Jellyby's "telescopic philanthropy" to the community around him, to his own particular here and now? Let him lay down his Magic-Markered histories and atlases, go out his front door, and take a stroll to, say, the V.A. hospital at 50 Irving Street. Let him walk through it during visiting hours; the patients—some of them abandoned by their women when their capacities as (wonderful word, this) "providers" were suddenly curtailed by a grenade or a bullet—will probably be glad of the company. There he will find floor after floor of people with limbs amputated, eyes put out, innards scrambled, bodies broken—virtually all of them men, virtually all of them there *because they are men.*

Am I getting through? That is—and I'm going to repeat this, in hopes that it may penetrate, even to readers in Washington—he will find the male forty-nine percent of his fellow citizens selectively registered, regimented, brutalized, and exposed to shot and shell according to a social contract so pervasive, and until recently so widely accepted as natural law by both men and women (and even now reaffirmed by Court and Congress), that people like Mr. Palmer, their faraway gaze following Mrs. Jellyby's to seek out the horrors of other lands in other ages, still cannot perceive its ubiquitous casualties.

Let Mr. Palmer, standing in the middle of his maimed and dying brothers, meditate on the fact that some feminists, incensed over such atrocities as Tanzanian infibulations, technicolor representations of repetitive heterosexual fellatio, and pay toilets (which oppress women because women can't use urinals), and convinced that on some profound level all these outrages are part of one sinister pattern, consider veterans' benefits a patriarchal perk and want them cut or cut back. Let him then leave these privileged phallocrats and take a look-in at Arlington Cemetery, where the real power elite is, and then round out his Cook's tour of the master sex with a visit to some of his city's jail cells, drunk tanks, drug-detoxification centers, or charity wards, where he will find yet more men, doubtlessly worn out after a hard day of mutilating female genitals and administering unnecessary radiation, doing an awfully good job of imitating the wretched of the earth.

The trouble with man's lot today is not that men have been raised to be stoics, but that they have been given so much to be stoical about. They commit suicide at such a disproportionate rate because, on the whole, the arrangement they have made with the other half of humanity winds up giving more of them good reason to. Today's Jellybys—whose wonderful capacity for not seeing whatever most pertains to themselves simply illustrates their complicity in the arrangement—are products of the old deal, according to which the women were to refrain from thinking (thus producing Andrea Dworkin) and the men from feeling. The new deal, if it is to come in earnest, must sometime soon absorb the news that both prohibitions are passé.

That means, first of all, that women seeking liberation have simply got to drop the sisterhood-is-powerful, united-front line and start letting the loonies, dummies, drivelers, and poison-penners among them know that, though they're welcome to stay on as troops, they won't get to play spokesperson anymore. (What is appalling about *Against Our Will* is not that one woman wrote it but that so many women read it.)

It means, also, abandoning the trendy atavism that at the moment seems to be getting more popular all the time, and becoming reconciled to the rigors of reason—facing the fact, for instance, that nothing short of nuclear war can reduce the earth's population to the half-billion people capable of being sustained should the phallic machines and systems be abandoned. It may be too bad, but the human race some time ago passed the point of no return: Thinking got us into this, and thinking is going to have to get us out.

As for men, their need right now is not for the much-vaunted right to cry, but simply for the capacity to get very damned angry at what is being said about them as a sex, and at the everywhere-manifest consequences of the propaganda. I confess to finding it rather chilling that a man can read something like *Gyn/Ecology* or *The Women's Room,* or put up with the attitudes that such books feed, in a state of bored acquiescence or even sympathy. It is as if a Jew were to read through *Mein Kampf* taking notes on the imagery. I think about these men—the ones who gave the rave reviews to *Of Woman Born;* a former colleague of mine, whose name I had probably better not give, who during the very week the Congress was passing the all-male draft registration bill saw fit to show his opposition to sexual discrimination by protesting a stripper's presence on campus; a *New York Times* book reviewer puffing a book whose thesis is that he is the scum of the earth ("Again! Whip me again!") —and I stand amazed. There is a kind of almost supernatural obtuseness in these men that at times can become, as the statistics reveal, literally suicidal.

As of now, men are the only minority in the country for whom the kind of special pleading made incessantly by their enemies is actually applicable. Of what other group could Justice Rehnquist have declared, in a majority opinion, that its right not to be singled out by the government for harassment, servitude, and the threat of death was a "facile abstraction"? What other group has had its collective sense of self-interest so cauterized that it could hear these words spoken about itself without thronging by the millions into Washington to hang Justice Rehnquist from the portico of the Supreme Court Building?

Justice Rehnquist obviously knows whose ox to gore. Members of the Supreme Court, as everyone knows, read the newspapers. They are well aware that at the moment they inhabit a country where men are uniquely the targets of a flood of fashionable hate literature that goes unchecked and unchallenged, a country where, for instance, a man will without complaint take upon himself the tedious business of driving (and look out the window, at how many of the cars with couples in them have men in the driver's seats, if this observation sounds dated to you) and then get glowered at if at the end of the trip he thoughtlessly tries to hold the car door open for his passenger, a country where, for all the fine "fifty-fifty" talk of the last several years, men in divorce cases are still routinely deprived of their children and saddled with supporting them *in absentia.*

So men should not wonder at the Court's latest official affirmation of the Montagu Doctrine. They should not scratch their heads and ask how the same Court, having proclaimed for years the unconstitutionality of legislative discrimination, could then declare, in *Weber* v. *United Steelworkers of America,* that, on second thought, when it comes to employment practices, discriminating against men is all right; and then declare, in *Michael M.* v. *Superior Court,* that, come to think of it, when it's a matter of criminal cases, discrimination against men has something to be said for it; and then declare, in *Rostker* v. *Goldberg,* that, hey, you know, when it comes to life and liberty, discrimination against men is not such a bad idea. How can they get away with that? Because you let them, my man.

What's needed is not crying but yelling, a certain amount of undignified and unmanly squeaking-wheel-ery, until Justice Rehnquist and his brethren and their coequals in the other branches of government are put on notice that they can't pull that kind of shit anymore.

There may once have been a time when men would have been allowed to feel some kind of compensatory self-affirmation from the excess weight loaded on their shoulders—but you can forget about that now, sucker. Ask a Vietnam veteran how affirmed he felt when he figured out that he had been sold the moral equivalent of the Brooklyn Bridge. And listen to my old friend Mira, would you? Remember that old Freudian question, *"What does woman want?"* Listen to Mira, and the answer comes clear: *Whatever she can get.* It's time that you, and your brothers, learned that lesson from her.

5

Juno's Legions

The women were over-excited, and when I tried to talk to them they crowded round me and began jeering and shrieking at me because I am not married. A dozen screamed at a time, and so rapidly that I could not understand all they were saying, yet I was able to make out that they were taking advantage of the absence of their husbands to give me the full volume of their contempt.

John Millington Synge,
The Aran Islands

FOR most of us in our daily lives, the Montagu Doctrine has most commonly manifested itself in the convention that anything bad with women is the fault of men. That was what the older Victorian gentleman of L.P. Hartley's *The Go-between* was saying when he explained firmly, "Nothing is ever a lady's fault," and what the generation ahead of mine conveyed with the expression "the better half." It is the assumption behind this dialogue from *The Women's Room,* between a woman inmate in an insane asylum and her visitor:

"Those women," Mira nodded to the departing figures. "Are they guests?"

"Oh, no. They're like me." Lily laughed. "What this place really is is a country club for women whose husbands don't want them anymore."

Mira looked around. That sounded like Lily's insanity, but almost everyone around them was female, between thirty and fifty.

"Aren't there any men?"

"Oh, yes, but they're mostly old alcoholics."

"Are there old alcoholic women too?"
"Yes, lots of them. We're all people nobody wants."

Anyone familiar with the literature knows at this point that the "we" of this passage—the ones driven to drink by heartless rejection—are the women; the men, meanwhile, remaining just what they look like, "old alcoholics." Alcoholism is traditionally a male problem, insanity (although the movement is divided on this subject, one side's figures showing that most asylum inmates are female, thus showing how brutalized women are; the other's figures showing that most inmates are male, thus showing how unfit men are) a female problem; ergo, lunatics on the whole deserve compassion, but drunks do not, exceptions being made of course for female drunks.

The feminist formula justifying this old chivalric hangover has remained virtually unchanged since it was voiced in 1969 by Kate Millett in *Sexual Politics:* "As both the primitive and the civilized worlds are male worlds, the ideas which shaped culture in regard to the female were also of male design. The image of women as we know it is an image created by men and fashioned to suit their needs."

Now, I would like to suggest to the reader that just because you hear this all the time in one form or another does not mean that it is true. Leaving aside, for the time, the question of just what Millett means by primitive and civilized "worlds"—"world" being a mighty big word—try asking yourself whether you yourself have been shaped exclusively according to male design.

First, there was your mother, that figure with whom most of us spend most of our first five years. Was she an insignificant influence on your "image"? (Or is it that she is supposed to have passed on patriarchal values beaten into her in *her* infancy? Beaten into her by whom? Her mother? Then where did *those* come from? *Somewhere* along the line there has to be an identifiable male to blame things on.) Then, if you had a typical education, like mine, for instance, your first six to nine years of school were under the tutelage of women. And speaking for myself, the six women who guided me through grade school—the sweetheart, the sadist, the pusher, the big sister, the card, the pill—remain among the vividest fixtures of my memory.

Then, just about the time the average youngster begins to leave behind this succession of women guardians, what should hit him or her, like a piano dropped from some invisible fortieth floor, but adolescence. And adolescence happens to be, as far as the relations between the sexes is concerned, a gynocracy. As everyone agrees—or at least as everyone agreed when *I* was an adolescent—girls at this stage are maturing faster than boys, which is to say they've figured out the score sooner than the boys have. The pretty ones figure out that they are pretty, and, the better to reinforce that impression and so augment their power over the males, commence the systematic avoidance of their less attractive friends and cultivation of their more attractive ones. They set up, within their own ranks, an elaborate hierarchy of desirables, undesirables, and untouchables, whose influence extends to male society as well: For all practical purposes, the word "turkey" (or whatever the equivalent is now) can be translated as "a boy spurned by influential girls."

Of course the influence is to some degree reciprocal, and of course there is plenty of carnage on both sides. The fact remains that adolescence is, on the whole, a period when the average young man emerges from the custodianship of older women into a social world where, more than ever before, the females have the upper hand. The two things that matter most to an adolescent are status and sex. As for status, the teen-age girl's greater proficiency in its mysteries is largely what we mean when we say she is more mature than her male counterpart; as for sex, the girl suddenly finds herself in the position of a molybdenum magnate in a wildly inflated strategic metals market: Something of no apparent intrinsic value has overnight given her immense power over half the people she knows. She herself is anything but immune to the condition, but her feelings are more easily deflected or diffused into fantasy—into crushes on rock stars and teachers, for instance—or atomized into vague visions in a way that usually frees her to do a certain amount of calculating even when clinching with her probably not-so-fantastic male friends. (I say nothing, here, about whether this difference is natural or cultural, just that it is, or anyway was, real.)

Seen as a power struggle, the contest between men and women at this point isn't even close: The woman has more leverage and more skill at using it; the man, starting by this point to hear rumors of how it's supposed to be a man's world out here, finds that his options are in effect limited to two—he can ask women out and play by their rules, or he can stay home and masturbate. (Some world.) No wonder feminist fiction so often seems arrested in this period—its men maladroit, crude, obnoxious, socially retarded, grotesquely oversexed, as adolescent boys really are; its women regal questers and visionaries keeping them at arm's length: It is simply a projection, into adult life, of realities remembered from that time when women are most in charge—from, that is, the time most approximating the ideal feminist state of nature.

This embarrassing fact, that most of us grow up in a world dominated by females, is one big reason for the feminist fixation on the media. *Something* has to be turning these momma's darlings into the chauvinist pigs they mostly become; and if, according to the Millett gloss of the Montague Doctrine, it can't be the mommas themselves, it must be something outside their control: *not* the fathers—one of the major complaints being that fathers aren't involved enough as it is in their children's training —so that leaves that other family member, the television set, preaching its sexist gospel in the father's place.

But of course the television repertoire, especially at the hours when young children are usually watching it, is much more likely to reflect than to contradict the mother's values. Television is essentially the sum product of many well-paid and highly intelligent individuals' efforts to figure out what the average woman wants to hear and tell it to her—woman, not man, because women do most of the shopping. If the polls showed that the mothers of America wanted their daughters to be aggressive and their sons to be gentle, television could be counted on to trip over its tongue in its haste to deliver the message to their children. I understand that in a few ways it is indeed starting to change the ways it shows women to themselves—here a superwoman, there an anchorperson—from which we may conclude that in a few ways women have changed how they like to think of themselves. The fact remains that now, as in the past, television is one more female influence in the predominantly female world that baby, child, and teen-ager inhabit. Male or female, he or she reaches adulthood equipped with a woman's version of the way to be.

That is of course most obviously true in the case of a female. The way that teen-age girls keep one another in line, especially in the battle plan for their dealings with boys, is something that, twenty years later, I still remember with pity and terror. James Thurber writes somewhere of a man who inadvertently witnesses the once-over head-to-foot look that one attractive young woman can give a possible rival and runs off to a desert island, so horrifying has been his glimpse into the depths of human nature. I have seen that look; I can understand how that man feels. I can also remember the way in which that Sicilian sisterhood, the teen-age clique, deals with its black sheep.

We hear a lot these days about locker-room talk, in which males punctuate their comparisons of penis size and cement their bondings by traducing female reputations. Well, I am a male whose pathetic lifelong effort to get into shape has taken him in and out of locker rooms for the past twenty-plus years, and I would like to record that the last time I heard one of those talks was during my senior year of high school. I would also like to record my vivid recollection from high school—that "reputation" is a female word in the same way and to the same extent that "halfback" is a male word.

To be sure, it was the boys who went around claiming to have deflowered each entire female freshman class within a month of its arrival, but it was the girls who spread the word about which stories could be believed. They were the impresarios of reputation, the arbiters and the enforcers, the stoolies and the goons, the commodities marketeers exchanging tips and newsletters on (more female words) who was cheap and fast; nice and not nice; who was a tease and who a whore; who was cheating or running around.

Germaine Greer in *The Female Eunuch* remembers it the same way: "The most scathing vilification of immoral women does not come from men. The feminine establishment which sees its techniques of sexual bargaining jeopardized by the disregard of women who make themselves *cheap* is more vociferous in its condemnation."

The boys in their locker-room talks were never better than pensioners on female patronage—which may be one reason why most of them cut it out on leaving high school. It may also be a reason why many girls never do cut it out—why throughout their adult lives so many women continue to lay down the law to one another, and to put up with its being laid down.

Because from what I can see, the portioning of relationships into good and bad remains, long after high school, a largely female enterprise. My friend Neil likes to say that the Olympic officials faced with the distasteful job of determining which of those East European entrants in female competitions are really female could save themselves a lot of trouble simply by showing each contestant a picture of an old man paired with a woman young enough, as they say, to be his daughter: "If the words 'No fool like an old fool' come uncontrollably, reflexively, from the mouth, it's definitely a woman."

At least as much as the breach in ranks represented by the girl who puts out too soon, the threat represented by an older man's liaison with a younger woman is something that women seem especially anxious to single out and thunder at. Even a book like *The Women's Room,* which sports its sexual liberation like a Jacobin's rosette and which in most ways is a pure fictional distillation of the Montagu Doctrine, can't refrain from asides at "the town pump" and the "little chippies" whom men, having (yet another female term here) "no standards," run after.

I read in the paper that all this is in the process of being changed, and I hope it's true. But my own observations, I'm afraid, still square with those of Anne Taylor Fleming, who noticed that when the saga of Mary E. Cunningham's rise and fall at the Bendix Corporation was in the news, women were the ones rushing to judgment. In a *New York Times Magazine* article she writes:

. . . it was women, other successful women, who were often quicker than men to ascribe that rise to her blond beauty and to her inferred romance with Bendix chairman William M. Agee. I heard these women, at parties, in restaurants, wellaccoutered in their gabardine suits and gold chains, hint, in well-bred innuendoes, that Miss Cunningham had used her sexuality to get ahead. She was too young, they said wistfully, too lovely, they said enviously, not to have. Her resignation from Bendix they took as confirmation of their suspicions.

The eighteen-to-twenty-one-year-olds I see in my course entitled "The Battle Between the Sexes" agree: One almost unanimous conclusion to emerge from discussions has been that although distinctions between men and women have dissolved to the point where each sex discusses the other in pretty much identical terms (one girl who rode back to school on the football-team bus remarked that the language she heard there about girls was exactly the same that her friends used to talk about boys), when it comes to discussing members of their own sex, females are still the hardballers, hands down. A confused young man—confused because as a child of the Seventies he has been raised not to notice such things—records what my generation took for granted:

My friend and I were saying how much we like our economics professor. We were commenting on her teaching methods. The girls who were there disagreed with us, saying how much they hated her. They felt the reason we like her was because she was young and pretty. I almost started crying. I laughed so hard. I told them that I hardly found her attractive. Then they both started talking about every detail of the lady's appearance, from her haircut to her shoes. I couldn't believe it.

A young woman in the same course, reporting on the life of a female scorekeeper for a baseball team, illustrates the same point:

These scorekeepers fall into three generally recognized categories: the girlfriend, the desperate one, and the slut. . . . [The girlfriend] is a girl who has a boyfriend on the team and is keeping the scorebook solely for seeing him play, while getting free rides to and from the games. The girlfriend score-keeper is rarely faced by problems from either sex and is more often trusted by them. Some players see her as a Dear Abby or a mother-figure and confide in her, usually about their own girlfriends. The usually-jealous females in the stands know that the girlfriend scorekeeper is already attached, therefore not a threat, and they accept and also confide in her easily. . . .

The desperate ones are in the majority and, generally, are unattractive and fat, haven't had much dating experience, and are not well liked. The desperate scorekeeper is the source of much ridicule from both sexes, especially the female spectators, who hold no compassion for her. They pick on her personality and appearance and make her the subject of many malicious jokes. The girls in the stands discuss her previous boyfriends, if she has had any, and they are nasty purely for the benefit of their female egos. . . .

The conflict between the slut and the jocks is not as bloodthirsty as that between the slut and the other females. . . . Every girl who has a boyfriend on the team would like to kill the slut. The girls constantly talk about her and are suspicious of her every move. They denounce her figure, her hair, her clothes, and anything else they can find to pick on. . . . Any player who has a girlfriend in the stands knows better than to give the slut anything more than his name, position, or batting average, or he'll catch hell from his girlfriend, who's sure to be watching his every move. If the slut happens to be pretty or have a nice personality, proving to be a threat to the girlfriends, they can get madder and more ruthless than an umpire arguing a call with Billy Martin.

This last comment shows that the author knows less about baseball than she does about sexual politics—about which she is, I fear, quite perceptive. She says that's the way it is, and I know for a fact that that's the way it was. At least up until marriage, of the four possible discharges of influence among the sexes—men influencing men, men influencing women, women influencing men, women influencing women—the last is without question the most pressured, the most relentless, the most totalitarian. Back in the prefeminist days, when women would admit this sort of thing, one of marriage's main attractions for a woman was often simply the fact that it allowed her to partially escape the claustrophobic company of other women.

Second only to the female influence on other females is the female influence on males. The Montagu Doctrine as preached by feminists holds of course that women's influence on men extends only to the ways in which men can be said to be better than they would otherwise have been. But I've been there, and I remember different. So, I'm happy to say, does Ingrid Bengis in her (almost uniquely) honest feminist memoir, *Combat in the Erogenous Zone:* "The woman I am remembers a time in our not-so-remote history when American women (myself included) were objecting to the fact that American men were not as virile or gallant as their European counterparts; remembers when no self-respecting Jewish girls wanted to have anything to do with nice Jewish boys."

Boy, do I remember that. I remember "Are you a man or a mouse?" I remember the litany of complaints about how men weren't virile or aggressive anymore, the way they were supposed to be. I remember that it was women who kept tabs on "who wears the pants" in which family, and I remember their scorn of any man who let himself be (another female word here) "henpecked" by one of their own. I remember the bumbling, apron-wearing Bumsteads of the comics (someone has done a survey showing that the husbands in midcentury comic strips were usually shorter than the wives) and the situation comedies that consisted of feckless old dad being humiliatingly buffaloed by the wife and kids, to peals of canned laughter. Above all, I remember that it was *women* who were telling you, over and over, to be a man, to take charge, to push them around ("I want a brave man, I want a caveman"), in language recently recalled to me by this letter in the newspaper:

Dear Ann,

For years I have been married to a weak, sissified wimp. I am almost sure he is bisexual, but I have no proof. This lily-livered twerp can't make a decision and won't stand up for himself. He is such a coward he embarrasses me.

And so on. Today, happily enough, such language sounds quaint (it comes from Ann Landers's column, that cryogenic repository of 1950s folk wisdom), but there was a time when it was the standard female idiom; with such terms was the whip cracked.

Why were women that way? Some of us wished we knew. We also wished they weren't that way—because, as it happens, there is no greater pain in the ass on God's green earth than someone who follows you around demanding that you *master* her. We had theories: that on some perverse level they saw bullying as an indisputable proof of attention; that they liked their men to be thuggish out of some plasmic memory of a time when a woman needed a good thug at her side to fend off saber-toothed tigers. Modern feminists, when they deign to deal with the issue, blame this rather nasty underside of the feminine mystique on Helene Deutsch—"a traitor to her own sex," Susan Brownmiller calls her—whose theories of female masochism they in turn blame on (you guessed it) Freud.

In any case, if a time-traveler from the 1980s had popped up around 1960 and started telling us that women were that way as a result of something called the "Stockholm syndrome," the process by which an oppressed class comes to love its chains, we'd have thought she was crazy. And we would have been right. Because there was not much about the women around us that suggested oppression, considering that in school they were usually the most successful students, and that out of school they finagled the social-sexual marketplace like so many natural-born Fisks and Goulds. If someone were going to talk about captives in chains, we might have said, here's a much better analogy for you: the eighteenth-century ladies and gentlemen of quality who used to enjoy watching the Bedlam lunatics rattle their manacles. Like Marie Antoinette and her ladies-in-waiting at the Petit Trianon, women as a group seemed to find it amusing to dabble in the primitive; they liked *un petit peu de sauvage* in their men for the reason that some people like their steak very rare, for the tingly whisper of blood amid the table linen and crystalware.

I speak as someone who learned the lesson, from women: Not too much polite, please. Please to beat your chest a bit. If you want to get laid, you've got to chase and you've got to push. Not too much—that's called "rape," and you'll live to regret it, boy—but enough to show you're serious.

I think my first inkling of the lesson came from the substitute teachers who occasionally took over class in my grammar-school years—sweet, harried, middle-aged ladies in suits and sensible shoes who were prone to while away the day by reading us sentimental poetry, and whose favorite poem always seemed to be "The Highwayman." (You know: "The highwayman came riding, riding . . . ") I think it may have been the recurring image of the innkeeper's daughter, tied to a bedpost, her breast blown up ("shattered" is the poem's memorable word) to warn off her outlaw lover, that first cued me to suspect that there was something a trifle *outré,* something not quite compatible with the Constitution and Bill of Rights, lurking in the vicinity of that baffling bloodroot, the female heart. It was dimly apparent to me then that the final tableau of a beautiful woman bound and gagged (for love!) with blood streaming down her nightgown (for love!) was very close to the center of whatever it was that made those ladies keep reading the thing to us.

The years after grammar school certainly confirmed the suspicion. Almost any man who grew to adulthood among women, in the years before feminism changed everything, knows what it's like, having to pretend to be that damned highwayman. The world—that large and confusing place full of things you don't understand and people who are one too many for you—is suddenly presumed to be a big machine that you, having after all been allowed the inestimable privilege of taking shop while the girls were taking home ec., ought to be able to take apart and put back together. If the headwaiter seats you next to the rest rooms, it's because you didn't do whatever it is men are supposed to do to make him respect you. If the car breaks down on the way home, you will of course stride manfully to the front, hoist up the hood or whatever it's called, and diddle the doohickeys until it's all better. We've been repeatedly urged, over the last few years, to feel sorry for women who, as a condition of the sexual contract, have had to repress and conceal their native capacities; well, I'm here to say that it's a hell of a lot harder pretending to be more competent than you arc than it is pretending to be less.

I remember, as one emblematic incident among many, visiting New York City for the first time in the company of a woman who had lived there all her life, asking her where we should go, and being told that I was the man and it was my decision to make. Now, my idea of New York at the time (I grew up in California) was what I had read in *Mad* magazine—that it was a place where everyone drank Moxie and used funny words like *chutzpah.* My idea of places to go in New York was pretty much limited to the Statue of Liberty and the Empire State

Building. I told her this, ironically. She answered, not ironically at all, that as a matter of fact she had never been to the top of the Empire State Building and that it sounded like a very interesting thing to do. The relationship didn't last long, but it served to crystallize for me what George Orwell had discovered when, as an imperial sahib, he found himself forced, by the combined will of a mob of silent Burmese, to shoot an elephant he did not wish to shoot—that "When the white man turns tyrant it is his own freedom he destroys."

The difference was that Orwell's Burmese weren't the ones who had made him into a sahib in the first place; they simply wanted him to faithfully act out the role he had assumed. Whereas in my experience, it was the women who established the roles, selling them to a gullible mankind by letting us play bwana from time to time.

Many of my memories of this setup involve cars, probably because I hate cars. Cars are to me by cultural fiat what Genesis says the pain of childbirth is to women by divine ordinance—a torment unfairly delegated to me because of my sex. To me, a car is ideally a large object —good when it works, bad when it doesn't—whose purpose in life is to take me from one place to another. I do not understand people who believe that the estate of manhood confers a moral obligation to go any further than that in my relation with cars—to actually get down in and explore, come to understand the workings of, these basically boring mechanical functionaries. Flushing a toilet, after all, does not confer upon one a moral obligation to master the sewage system.

Women, by and large, understand this, except that they persist in the convenient superstition that cars are one category of existence where it befits a man to display his famous mastery. I remember one automotive naïf whose main grievance against the lover she eventually dumped was that something was always wrong with his car, thus showing that he had not adequately come into man's estate. (That, plus the fact that, as she memorably put it—this was around 1970—"He's never going to earn more than ten thousand a year." Money-earning was another of those dreary mechanical fields that men were supposed to be good at.)

I remember another woman, in Boston, taking it personally when my car was towed by the Boston Police, and accompanying me to the station to vent her feelings. "Who do I make this check out to?" I asked. "To the Boston Police Department," the desk sergeant started to answer. "To the Boston Pigs," stage-whispered my friend, behind me, doubtless thinking to give me a chance to reestablish some of the manhood that in her view the tow truck had recently carted away. Let's you and him fight: *She* wasn't the one who was going to wind up behind bars.

I could go on—and on—but you get the idea. As far as I'm concerned, that's enough for now. How can they stand it, these women who write, or read, those weepy reams about all the ghastly mistakes they've made with the opposite sex? Like most of us, I've made some too; and I suppose in a less public forum, like a bar or a psychiatrist's office, there might be some therapeutic value to gushing them all out. But the thing is—and this is the point that keeps getting missed—it wouldn't *prove* anything for purposes of sexual politics, except for the obvious: that some women are nice and some aren't. Looking back, I can see plenty of incidents that could be used to illustrate the moral depravity of the female sex, but, honest to God, what a silly thing that would be to do. Silly, and fraudulent—because what would be required, more often than not, would be a certain amount of cropping and highlighting, a certain amount of cutting away what didn't fit.

Example (last one): I am visiting the city neighborhood of the woman I'm, as we put it, seeing. Since her mother disapproves of me (her daughter is Jewish; I'm not), we spend most of our time at a friend's family's apartment, where the plan is for me to spend the night. At about 10:00 P.M., the mother of this friend gets a phone call from mother number one, the one whose doorstep I'm not to darken. Said mother has just learned of other mother's intention of harboring me for the night. I believe that the word (shades of Susan Brownmiller on Helene Deutsch) "traitor" is used. In any case, I am forthwith informed that it's too bad but I can't spend the night after all, so strong is the bond of *Blutmutterschaft* invoked against me. I'm not trying to jerk tears, but the fact is that I was a college kid, with no transportation and almost no money, in the middle of a strange city whose streets are famous for being dangerous after dark, being thrown into the night by a regiment of women.

Well, there. Cut and print, and the moral is clear. Tell that kind of story twenty more times or so, string the stories together with a narrator who at the same time keeps meeting lots of really neat *men* who have been done in by their wives and mothers, and you have the makings of the antifeminist backlash confessional for which the *Zeitgeist* must by now, surely, be good and ready. But as it happened, the story didn't end there. Because my friend's friend, the daughter of the mother who was kicking me out, was appalled, and rallied around. She located a cot somewhere and set it up for me on the roof of the apartment building.

The rules of the genre—the genre being the getting-back-at-the-opposite-sex memoir—require that during the night the rains come down, or that I get mugged. But they didn't and I wasn't; the night was warm and clear, the stars twinkled, and in the morning the young woman who set up the cot tickled me awake and served me orange juice and toast while we watched one of the few sunrises it has ever been my privilege to see. A very nice memory, on the whole (and I hereby hoist my glass to you, Alexandra, should you come across these words out there somewhere, in appreciation of that morning on the roof), but pretty much useless as material for sexual ideology—its point being only that some women can be clods and some others can be dolls. What a boring point.

And I'm afraid that the same boring point is pretty much the sum and substance of what emerges when I review the men and women I've known, casually or intimately, throughout my life. Which leads me to suspect those, whether writers of fiction or writers of nonfiction, who come to radically different conclusions: I just don't believe that the apportionment of virtue between men and women is all that different in other places, or that it's changed that much in the past few decades. It is of course possible that some of these women have just been terribly unlucky, and deserve the pity they cry out for—but as freaks, not as types.

In any event, I do know that the one feminist memoir, whose sources I am in a position to compare with what the author made of them, has taken, as they say, certain liberties. It is Marilyn French's *The Women's Room,* which in 1977 simply put into parable what Kate Millett had declared in 1969—that men were in charge of everything and to blame for same; that whatsoever was wrong with women was the fault of men. And since, conveniently enough, *The Women's Room* has also been the most widely read and (probably) influential book to propagate this doctrine, it should be worthwhile to take a look at how honestly its exempla tally with the lives they come from.

Marilyn French and I both went through the Harvard English Department's Ph. D. program at the same time. We took some classes together, had some drinks together, both did our dissertations on James Joyce, knew many of the same people (including the women of the "women's room"), and in general were friendly (not anymore, boy) acquaintances. So when her book came out in 1977, I read it as a *roman à clef*, spurred on by the slight hope—or, after about page twenty (by which point it's clear that any man between *these* covers had better hold on to his tail), apprehension—that I might even recognize myself in it somewhere. (I didn't. Phew!) *The Women's Room* is a novel—which means that properly speaking it is entitled to do whatever it wants with the facts of its author's life—but at the same time it is a highly effective tract on behalf of the proposition that, to quote from its pages, "men are rotten and women are great." As such, it owes a good deal of its power to the author's insistence on having it both ways, on having us believe the essential truth of the yarns she's spinning:

You think I am making him up. You think, Aha! A symbolic figure in what turns out to be after all an invented story. Alack, alas, I wish he were. Then he would be my failure, not life's. I'd much prefer to think that Norm is a stick figure because I am not much of a writer than because Norm is a stick figure.

Technically speaking, this can be taken as just another fictive ploy—other novelists in the past have had their narrators swear up and down that we're getting the truth. What is different about *The Women's Room* is that, this time, people believed the narrator—so inured have we become recently to women's horror stories about themselves. Christopher Lehmann-Haupt, for one, quoted from the above passage in his *New York Times* review and allowed as how it did indeed undermine his sense that the book was fiction. And the other reviews were full of the same kind of thing: " . . . honesty . . . speaks from a place where every woman of us may have been but few have ever articulated . . . as raggedly true as life . . ."; " . . . honest . . . one cannot resist the novel's realism. . . ."; " . . . very real . . ."; "I know these women. . . . The characters in *The Women's Room* are my friends. . . ."; " . . . so filled with truth . . ."

Like Christopher Lehmann-Haupt, they all kept "forgetting that it was fiction." But fiction it was, compounded of fiction's usual mixture of life and legerdemain, plus this novel's one genuine innovation—that the author saw fit to tell the standard Galahad-versus-the-trolls story with a woman, *qua* woman, playing the part of Galahad, and men, very much *qua* men, taking the part of the trolls.

Now, if you were one of the millions who read the novel, and you took it as the standard feminist-opera-without-the-music and then put it down, fine. But if perchance you live under the delusion that a single one of its pages was at all related to the facts of the real world —and the reviews suggest that some people do sustain that delusion—then I'm here to say that I was there, and I have news for you. Or, at least, I have news about the Harvard sections: I didn't know Marilyn French before she arrived there, though I do note with interest that in the novel it is Mira's husband who walks out on her (thus showing what a cad he is), whereas according to newspaper interviews it was Marilyn who left her husband (thus implying what a loser he was).

Leaving that aside, let us take up the Cambridge section, beginning with the book's opening scene:

She climbed up the three flights of ancient, creaky stairs, reflecting that the ladies' room was in an inconvenient location because it had been added long after the building was erected. The school had been planned for men, and there were places, she had been told, where women were simply not permitted to go. It was odd. Why? she wondered. Women were so unimportant anyway, why would anyone bother to keep them out?

I can't remember whether those stairs are ancient and creaky (Sever Hall is an old building, all right), but I can confirm that they lead to the ladies', or women's, or whatever, room, in the basement. The reason I know that is that I have passed it, several times, on my way to the men's room, which is right next to it. It happens to be a fact that, in Massachusetts, almost all vintage educational facilities have their bathrooms, male and female, in the basement; indeed Boston schoolchildren customarily use the expression "May I go to the basement?" when they have to use the bathroom. The symbolic burial of women in the cellar at Harvard, or anywhere else, has nothing to do with it.

As for those places "where women were simply not permitted to go"—I don't know who could have told Mira about them, but in 1968, when the novel opens, they would have been lying. In 1968 I did hear rumors —perhaps from the same people who told them to Mira —that women were not allowed into the most remote dining area of the Harvard Faculty Club; but the first time I bravely marched into that region with a woman on my arm, I was seated without murmur, right next to a table full of women.

So much for the opening scene, from which the novel gets its title and, as we say in the lit. crit. business, its central metaphor. Here is a later exemplary passage— and note, please, the women's names here, remembering that the men all have names like "Norm" and "Hamp" and "Simp":

Kyla was twenty-four, Isolde, twenty-six, Clarissa, twenty-three. But Mira and I were thirty-eight, and Val was thirty-nine. . . . It is strange. All of us had lived much alone and had great confidence in our own perceptions, and were not used to being treated like fools, or patronized. When the [department representative] treated us like recalcitrant children, it made us very uncomfortable. But we didn't know what to do about it. . . . When you were finished and asked for recommendations, you got nice letters about your excellence as a mother figure, or your elderly stability.

Now, the person in question was without doubt one of the most widely detested individuals at Harvard University. He was, if memory serves, the star victim of a bloodcurdling murder mystery novel being compositely written, in a collective orgasm of getting-even fury, by one entire graduate class. The clear suggestion here that he was selectively boorish with women students is simply bogus; he was a bully, period, and, if anything, he preferred picking on men, like most bullies.

Then she came back and tried to get a job, but the market had dried up and nobody wanted to hire a woman over forty even if she had a Harvard degree. . . .

The market had indeed dried up in the mid-Seventies; but as it happened, things were somewhat less desperate for women—who were demanding and winning a nationwide policy of sexually discriminatory hiring, euphemistically called "affirmative action"—than for men. Mira might have had trouble getting a job, but her creator, Marilyn French, got one right away, as did every one of the women she wrote about who got their degrees and wanted jobs; some of the men did not fare so well. Reverse discrimination, incidentally, continues apace in the academic job market. It is not uncommon for male candidates to be told frankly that, in the code words of the day, "other things being equal," the job will go to a woman. Then they go home to their graduate-school garrets and read about how women are their victims.

The handling of the events and main characters is of a piece with the rest of the novel: Toward the end of the book, eight radical feminist women attempt to rescue a persecuted sister from jail and are all killed by machine-gun-wielding policemen; the closest thing to such an incident, during the years covered, was the holdup of a Boston-area bank by a band of Brandeis students, during which none of the women bandits were killed but a male police officer was. The character Harley (Harley!), who in the novel is a philistine physicist given to macho put-downs of his wife Kyla (Kyla!) and her fellow humanists as arty butterflies, was in actual fact a poet.

But enough. Any more of this kind of thing would be irrelevant, anyway, to anyone who understands the first thing about fiction—the first thing being, to be precise, that it is not true.

For the others—those who were suckered into thinking that *The Women's Room* and other books like it were telling them something "honest" and "realistic" and "real" and "filled with truth"—well, shame on them. It's clear that they have let feminism's trendy resurrection of the Montagu Doctrine blind them to what normally they would recognize as yet another illustration of an old established truth of human nature: that people who complain excessively about the rest of humanity are telling us more about themselves than they are about the rest of humanity; and that those who single out one class or race or sex for abuse (they're called, except when they're feminists, "bigots") are the most self-revealing of all. Women who tell you that all men are Nazis, like men who tell you that all women are ball-busters, are talking mainly about themselves.

Exhibit A, again from Marilyn French:

You know how you feel when someone whispers to you that so-and-so is ill and you say, "Too bad," and ask what the matter is and they whisper "Women's troubles"? You never pursue it. You have this vague sense of oozings and drippings, blood that insists on pouring out of assorted holes, organs that drip down with all the other goo and try to depart, breasts that get saggy or lumpy and sometimes have to be cut off. Above all there is the sense of a rank cave that never gets fresh air, dark and smelly, its floor a foot thick with sticky, disgusting mulch.

Hold your gorge; there's more later in the book:

"The real reason is sanitary. You let women through front doors and what will they do? Splat splat, a big clot of menstrual blood right on the threshold. Every place women go they do it: splat splat."

And yet again, later:

Those stained sanitary napkins, those bloody underpants were hers, she knew they were hers, and she knew the men would know it too. She tried to stand in front of them, but there was no way she could conceal them.

And, for good measure, from her *New York Times* interview with Nan Robertson:

"He [a Catholic priest who had asked her advice on whether women students needed special treatment during their periods] saw little clots of menstrual blood under every one of those chairs."

The name for this phenomenon is "projection," and I've yet to find a feminist tract that is not transparently a case study: Mary Daly exorcising, with imprecations against the "Torture Cross Society," her girlhood as a good, pious, sentimental Catholic; Adrienne Rich, in and out of hospital and suffering from arthritis, spinning out her paranoid historical nightmare about how all doctors hate women; Susan Brownmiller, writer, shrieking down, for hundreds upon hundreds of pages, the Susan

Brownmiller, adolescent, who used to swoon over Ayn Rand's rape fantasies; Kate Millett's droning dialogue of one with the woman in her who used to be crazy about D.H. Lawrence.

The "Dedication" to Diane Wakoski's *Motorcycle Betrayal Poems* says it all, I'm afraid: "This book is dedicated to all those men who betrayed me at one time or another in hopes they will fall off their motorcycles and break their necks." To which the only reasonable response, of course, is that women who are attracted to the type of men who ride motorcycles (Wakoski's book was published before motorcycles became bourgeois) can expect to get betrayed a good deal; and that the woman whose ideal of the male mystique is a motorcycle gang can expect to get kicked around a good deal; and that in any case it's her problem.

Has anyone noticed that the works most singled out for feminist fury—Rousseau, Lawrence, the Bible itself —are precisely those works that, in the past, women have most made their own? (The first example of this I know of is Harriet Beecher Stowe's *Lady Byron Vindicated,* which is very savage indeed toward another old favorite with the ladies, Lord Byron.) In fact, most of feminism's stock villains are simply straw effigies, with male faces, representing ideas and feelings that liberated women no longer wish to entertain. Phyllis Chesler, Susan Brownmiller, and others get a good deal of mileage out of the fact that the Rolling Stones, for instance, are men, singing songs about abusing women, as if that proves something about men—but of course anyone familiar with popular culture knows that the Rolling Stones are mainly a female phenomenon, singing mostly to young women. In relation to the male sex, the Rolling Stones are just five unusually talented, unusually disgusting middle-aged men. In relation to the female sex, they are, I'm afraid, a fixture we've seen before—that damned highwayman still riding, riding. And it isn't the fault of men if he won't go away.

So the major feminist debate—and this fact is increasingly becoming unignorable—is not between men who want women to be a certain way and women asserting their right to be otherwise, but between two competing groups of women over the proper role of their own sex, and to a great extent of the other sex as well—with men, for the most part, just waiting for the dust to settle so they can go with the winner. And it was ever thus. Mixed society is a predominantly female institution, following rules set by women—"ladies," they used to insist you call them, as they now insist you don't, with most men, as usual, only trying to give them whatever the hell it is they want.

Nowhere is this more obvious than in the repeated complaint about being exploited as sex objects, a complaint that amounts, when all is said and done, to women who read *Vogue* being heckled by women (sometimes the same women) who read *Ms.*, with men being positioned in the line of fire. Because the decision that women shall be sex objects has been largely a female one. Men, knowing a good thing when they see it, have occasionally tried to work the same trick for themselves, but with very limited success. Women, so far, have been the only ones able to muster the sangfroid and esprit de corps required to make oneself simultaneously as desirable and as remote as possible, for the purpose of getting something extra in what would otherwise be an even exchange. They are to be congratulated, grudgingly, on their mastery of sexual realpolitik; and if they ever decide to give it up for real, they are to be congratulated on their generosity; but in any case, one thing they're not entitled to is indignation about the terms of the arrangement.

My friend Neil invented a parable, one evening, about that arrangement. "Imagine," he said, "what it would be like if the earth were to pass through some comet or radiation belt or whatever, so that the ecosystem got altered in peculiar ways, and one of the ways was that every sexually active male woke up the next morning with this incredible lust to fondle the female elbow. Nothing else—everything else was passé—just the elbow. What would happen? You know what would happen.

"Within a week, the women would have figured out what was going on, and they would have banded together for action. Wives waking up in bed next to husbands stroking their elbows and looking at them dreamily would talk to one another and put two and two together, and pretty soon the shit would really start to fly.

"The first thing to happen would be that full-length gloves would come back into fashion one day, and be *de rigueur* the next, and before you knew it women would be having one another arrested for not wearing them in the company of men. Genteel old gentlemen who didn't know what was going on would try to take a lady's arm to go across the street or into a dining room, and they'd get whacked with handbags and locked up. Bikinis would consist of two chic little armlets. The brassard would replace the brassiere. The same mothers who used to teach their daughters always to sit with knees locked together, because men were only interested in *one thing,* would call them back and retool them to walk around with their arms *high* and *back,* and pretty soon a roomful of women would look like a flock of geese about to take off. Or better yet, they would teach them to walk around with their arms straight down at their sides, thus minimizing the elbows as much as possible.

"Women in bars would insist that they be served drinks with super-long straws, so they could drink them right from the counter and not have to do any—you should excuse the expression—elbow bending. Nuns would wear casts. Novices would wear splints. Teen-age girls in the back seats of cars who weren't in the mood would start fending off their boyfriends with their boobs.

"The fashion industry would be revolutionized, cranking out elbow bandages made of ermine and lace, with daring little peekaboo numbers for evenings out and sensible plaid swatches for the office, and the length of upper and lower arm would go up and down, possibly in phase with the stock market.

"Some women might learn to walk on their hands, with their skirts falling down over their faces, for which they would cut portholes. Being multiorgasmic would go out and being double-jointed would come in.

"My old nemesis, Mrs. Weatherwax, would be off somewhere telling a new sorority of recruits that you have to draw the line somewhere and that as far as she was concerned anything above the wristwatch was no-man's-land. The fast girls would be the ones who let you tickle the insides of their arms on the first date, and the ones trying to hold the line would tell everyone that they didn't mean to be catty or anything but frankly, my dear, everyone knows that so-and-so bends like a pretzel.

"Needless to say, shameless hussies would start turning up in Times Square, flashing their flexors at the male passersby and promising more to anyone with the time and money; and needless to say, there would suddenly be tons of feminist tomes about how these hussies were being exploited by brutal male fascist capitalist lust, and about how eons of patriarchal elitism had trained men to think they could get away with fondling the elbows of women with whom they had not established a meaningful relationship, by which these tomes would mean marriage.

"Because, you know, that's what's really happened. Who knows when? I don't, but I know it definitely happened. Maybe it was back in the pre-whatever period, when the males were out on the veld, trying to round up the daily auroch, and the females were sitting around back at the camp, grinding the daily millet, and one of them told the other about how she had gotten Og to give her her new pelt, and one of those big light bulbs lights up above the heads of the assembly, which changes everything forever. And womp, there you have it: a sit-up strike, and God help the scabs. *Lysistrata* has the right idea, except it's got it backward: It should be first the embargo, then the war, and the war was over the first controlled substance, the original restricted commodity and cornered market, which was the female bod, as hoarded, bonded, hyped, bartered, and rationed by the female brain."

So Neil. I have in my files a news clipping—an article by Steven Krasner—that illustrates nicely the arrangement Neil describes. It is about the controversy surrounding the recent cover of the magazine *Women's Sports.* The cover shows an attractive young woman athlete wearing a low-cut top. Writes one angry subscriber: "The fact that you have a sexy marathon runner on the cover of the April issue indicates to me that you are not yet ready to cover and write about women's sports, and I am not happy that I have just renewed my subscription. In a male-dominated magazine I would label your attitude chauvinist, but I am at a loss to know what to call it in a female publication."

What is interesting, and what seems to indicate that Neil's little elbow fable involves a good deal of truth-telling, is the editor's defense: "If we were on more newsstands, then I think the criticism might be valid. But 80 percent of our sales are subscriptions. It isn't that we're just trying to attract male readers, though we do have some male readers. We have 105,000 subscribers, and I'd say 90 percent of those are women." Also, "Our

complete editorial staff is all women." It is, exactly, the
Judy Chicago criterion again: *Men aren't involved.*

What would make the cover "chauvinist" would be
the possibility that some men might view it with pleasure
while hurrying past a newsstand on their proper business
of earning the missus a new pelt. It is the same principle
that is at work when Robin Morgan (in *Going Too Far*)
pauses, before starting to give us her account of female
rape fantasies, to fret about whether some males might
be in the audience:

> . . . the certainty that they wait like spectators in the arena
> drooling over their ices and settling down on their cushions
> *is* unsettling for those who, no matter how well trained for the
> encounter, emerge to confront and wrestle with the newly
> uncaged beasts. Most absurd of all is the notion that one is
> engaged in such an encounter for—oh hilarious thought—
> their entertainment.

Oh hilarious thought, indeed. What! Entertain men
while edifying one another? Ha ha. In return for *nothing?*
Ha ha *ha.* The principle is as clear as can be: "Nix Sex
to Get Respect," reads the headline of an Ann Landers
column, which goes on to elaborate: "I'm not saying all
guys are skunks, but most of them will take anything they
can get. And why not? What do they have to lose? Your
body belongs to you. You don't owe anybody trespassing
privileges. . . ." Unless he comes across with that little
ring, that is.

The evidence, as far around as you can see or as far
back as you can read in history, is overwhelming: The
"exploitation" of women, the practice of "cheapening"
(consider the metaphor) and making an "object" of the
female body, is a business largely initiated and maintained by women. Distasteful or ludicrous or irksome as
some of them may have found it in the past, they have

realized how important that business is for maintaining their power. And that power, *pace* Susan Brownmiller *et al.,* has been formidable.

Two of the consequences of this power are prostitution and pornography, which many women in general and feminists in particular wish to repress for the same reason that moves Chrysler Corporation to request tariffs against Toyotas: "Of all the reactions women had to pornography," writes Susan Quinn of a survey done for *Glamour* magazine, "the most common was the fear that their bodies were being compared unfavorably to those of the nudes in the photographs." "I don't want my guy being turned on by anyone but me," explains one woman frankly. "When I look at those girls in the skin mags, I compare my body to theirs." Another reaches instinctively for one of those mercantile-ideological words that feminists have substituted for the old vocabulary of sin and purity: The more pornography she encountered, she writes, "the more I began degrading myself. My self-image crumbled. . . . Our relationship is back to normal, but my pride in my looks never returned." And yet another: "My husband's favorite parts of the female body are the breasts—the bigger, the better. This intimidates me tremendously because I am very thin and flat-chested, more the model type."*

That is the sad, seamy story behind all the cant about exploitation and degradation. Men might just as reason-

---

*Which anxiety explains, no doubt, the otherwise unaccountable predilection of women's fashion magazines for the boyish and the cadaverous in their models. As for men, someday someone is going to figure out that the mammary fixation of skin magazines derives not from oral infantilism—a theory with obvious appeal to miffed women—but from the fact that enlarged breasts are the main sign to a boy who has just hit puberty that the girl in question has, too. It is nature's way of doing what teen-agers otherwise do for themselves by taking up smoking. The single biggest reason why women like to ogle the models in *Vogue* and men like to ogle the ones in *Playboy* is not that one sex is sexually childish and the other isn't, but that both sexes are sexually adolescent, and that as adolescents they were, as the cultural anthropologists would put it, imprinted differently. Anyway, remember you read it here first.

ably feel the same way, of course: "I sure as hell don't want my wife comparing me to that Harry Reams," said Neil to me, for obvious reasons, after he had seen *Deep Throat.* But he was joking, sort of, and those women surveyed by *Glamour* weren't. Women feel they have more to lose from such comparisons because they have arranged things so that they have more to gain when the game goes right.

It is all a question of competition, of supply and demand in a field in which women have long done everything they can to keep things as one-sided as possible. It is the inexorable logic that was responsible for the passing of the Comstock Laws, the Mann Act—all in response to largely female pressure—and in general the statutes designed to keep sexual gratification at a minimum and therefore at a premium, including those against free love, prostitution, pornography, and especially (Flo Kennedy and Bella Abzug, please note) birth control and abortion. As the feminist historian Sheila M. Rothman has observed in her excellent *Woman's Proper Place,* "It was women reformers and women physicians . . . who led a purity crusade that made the suppression of birth control information a major plank in the moral reform agenda," and who, as part of the same agenda, got the antiabortion laws on the books.

As for the traditionally female, recently feminist campaign against legalized prostitution, Kathleen Barry in *Female Sexual Slavery* gives the game away in an unguarded moment: "The 'service' provided in prostitution is not just traditional sex but the fulfillment of those sexual demands men cannot or choose not to fulfill in other areas of their life, with girl friend or wife. Their demand is for kinky or perverted and perhaps violent sex. (By "kinky or perverted" sex, Barry means, as anyone knows who has read anything about the prostitution business, blow jobs.)

THE **MYTH** OF THE **MONSTROUS MALE**

In a book by the Redstockings, who have an embarrassing way of cutting right to the heart of a matter, Barbara Leon cuts right to the heart of this one:

> Not the least of crimes committed against women under male supremacy is that of our emotional abandonment by men. Though it is harder to quantify than economic exploitation and less dramatic than physical brutalization, it is this central fact which is a prerequisite for all the other actions taken against us by our oppressors. It is also a starting point for understanding the currently fashionable "smash monogamy" line borrowed from the male left and the counter-culture: the "liberal," innovative wings of male supremacy. . . .
>
> "Smashing monogamy" is nothing new for men. They have been doing it for centuries.

That, finally, is what "oppression" means these days—"smashing monogamy" by abandoning or ignoring wives or girlfriends and allowing one's eye to rove. The Redstockings may be a fringe outfit, but when they speak of "the refusal to marry and the abandonment of women" as the center of all things "oppressive to women," they have defined precisely the way in which this middle-class, middle-of-the-road college student from one of my classes uses the word "suppress" in an excerpt from her journal: "Initially, I felt that the physical aspect of love (sex) would win his love. This was the beginning of my suppression. By giving of myself, I allowed him to have the dominant reign over the relationship. . . . Giving of myself in such magnitudes, I began to feel more and more suppressed and became less confident with myself."

Behind that young woman's sense that the mutual exchange of sexual pleasure is a process by which she gets suppressed is an unspoken conviction that she should be getting something extra out of the deal. Behind that conviction lie centuries of negotiations between men and women in which the woman's claim to something extra —marriage or money or both—was understood.

Feminists are fond of saying that men have projected their own schematic, either-or assumptions on women by dividing them all into whores and madonnas, but in fact the evidence shows that if anything it has been women who have worked this number on themselves, as part of the business of pricing themselves as high as possible.

For one thing, they do it to men as well (just about any man knows that to be told by a woman that she thinks of you as a friend she respects is to be told to keep your hands to yourself). Beyond this, it has been women who have been the major proponents of female chastity, delicacy, and frigidity, and one inevitable consequence of the campaign has been that those women who won't or can't play along with the madonna *shtik* are extravagantly devalued, into whores. Madonna or whore, a woman playing by the rules of her own sex is equally a sex object, as defined mainly by herself and her fellow women: One inevitable derivative of the statement "I'm saving myself for marriage" is the proposition "I am, my 'self' is, a cunt."

The feminist position on these disagreeable facts is that women have been forced to withhold and barter their bodies in exchange for power because, as members of Kate Millett's primitive and civilized "male worlds," they haven't been allowed any other way of getting it. They have had to adopt the essentially reactive and defensive *Lysistrata* strategy as a way of winning a few rights back after the male usurpation of total power.

The argument makes sense up to a point. Yes, that trade-off probably has been the cornerstone of whatever rough parity the sexes have worked out. On the other hand, there is no reason whatever for thinking that men fired the opening shot, to which women responded in simple self-defense. That isn't the way things happen in

THE **MYTH** OF THE **MONSTROUS MALE**

life; there is no evidence for such a sequence in history
(which is one big reason for the feminist vogue in prehis-
tory); and myth, if anything, tells the opposite story, the
story of Apollonian males struggling to win their freedom from the earth mothers.

One myth, in particular, suggests that the traditional
female strategy of embargo, blackmail, and barter may
have been arrived at, with eyes open, as a deliberate
choice to claim certain privileges, even at the cost of
certain others. In his *Metamorphoses,* Ovid tells the story
of Tiresias, the only human to have been both a man and
a woman, being called before the gods on Olympus in
order to settle the argument over which sex gets more
pleasure out of intercourse. "Women," he answers without hesitation. ("Nine times as much," he adds in some
versions, which seems a bit excessive.)

Up to that point, the story makes a nice feminist fable
about woman's greater capacity for feeling and so forth
—and as such has been retailed, up to that point. But
what follows, and is usually edited out, is just as interesting: Juno, outraged that her secret has been revealed,
blinds and curses Tiresias, and sends him wandering
homeless through the world.

It isn't hard to understand her point of view. What,
after all, is likely to happen if Jupiter, and men in general,
figure out that the wives in their arms are experiencing
something more than the homely gratification of fulfill-
ing a duty? A lot of radical renegotiation, that's what. As
patroness of wives, Juno has a front to keep up, to which
the secret spilled by Tiresias has been absolutely essential.

The mythmakers knew what they were doing when
they made Juno the patroness of wives, eternally haggling with Jupiter when he felt in the mood for some
connubial cuddling amid the nimbi, eternally turning
into cows and whatnot the little chippies threatening her

monopoly. That has been the game plan, whence we have the madonna-whore business, which simply embodies the (mainly female) thesis and (mainly male) antithesis—what women assert about themselves and what men, largely in reaction, suspect. Elaine Morgan, whose *Descent of Woman* offers a brilliant and delightful, if slightly dotty, theory on the origins of this dialectic, understands very well the basic male attitude:

Somewhere in the very bottom layers of his consciousness is a deeply buried conviction that there is something prissy and phony about the way women carry on, and that if they weren't so damned hypocritical there should be times for every one of them—say one week in four—when she careered round the streets gaily admitting that she was mad for it, soliciting sex from all comers like a young howler monkey, and pursuing her prey until the sun went down and the men were all cowering exhausted in secret male hideouts.

Alas for Homo sap., we don't behave like that any more. We are not the match for him that we were originally designed to be. We chase after him for love, companionship, excitement, curiosity, security, a home and family, prestige, escape, or the joy of being held in his arms. But there still remains a basic imbalance between the urgency of his lust and ours, so that when it comes to the crunch the prostitute is always on a seller's market.

Morgan can keep her sense of humor because she believes that the rift occurred in the Pleiocene as a result of climatical developments that were nobody's fault. Would—to paraphrase somebody-or-other's words to John Paul Jones—that there were a thousand feminists like her.

But instead, this sort of thing, from Phyllis Chesler's *About Men,* is the norm: "Absurd as it is, men tend to use male sexual behavior as the ethic, the referent, for human (sexual) behavior. Men assume that if women were as 'free' as men, given the supposed sexual insatiability of women, they'd behave sexually like men. . . ."

Exactly. And men as a group have felt a lot more sure about that ever since that modern hermaphroditic Tiresias to whom Chesler here plays Juno, Masters-Johnson, let the cat out of the bag with their report on women's apparently awesome capacity for sexual response.

"After such knowledge, what forgiveness?" The jig is up. It turns out we men aren't the only horny little bastards in these parts. Although it is of course impossible for one man to speak for all men, I think it's safe to say that a popular saying back in the days when Neil and I were in college, that the ideal date was a nymphomaniac whose father owned a liquor store, was pretty close to the young-male consensus of the way things should be. Several years back, the trend-spotting magazines were suddenly full of articles about an epidemic of impotence among men disoriented by the new female aggressiveness, but the scare seems to have passed, and I suspect strongly that none of us need lose any sleep over that particular menace to the national well-being. Like women, men at times get jealous, or tired, or married, but the fact remains that, at least for a period, the average male's attitude toward sex is as innocent and simple (some would say childishly simple) as can be; viz., the more, the better.

Yeats's vision, in "Sailing to Byzantium," of an ideal sensuous realm of "the young in one another's arms" girdled by "the mackerel-crowded seas" is largely a *man*'s vision, as I discovered once when I used that expression, "mackerel-crowded seas," as a kenning for swinging singlehood to a woman friend then drifting from man to man. "Listen," she said to me, not joking, "I've spent some time in those mackerel-crowded seas, and some of the fish . . ." Her voice trailed off, the point

made, and so much for my half-serious reverie of a school
of dolphins—dolphins being known for their promiscuity, bisexuality, and randiness—twining themselves into
tingling tangles in the greeny deep, as a symbol for how
things could and should be on land.

Some of the fish in that aquatic garden of earthly delights were not so wonderous, she was reminding me;
here I'm thinking dolphins, and she's remembering the
crappies and the toadfish. And of course she was right—
God knows she was right—but what she was also telling
me was that to her that fact was of supreme importance.
And that was what distinguished us, and continues, so far
as I can see, to distinguish men and women.

A man who wakes up in the morning next to a stranger
he doesn't all that much care for in the light of day may
feel irked; he is not likely to feel wounded, used, or
devalued in some mysterious way or to resolve to himself, "Never again." ("Better luck next time" is what he
is likely to resolve to himself, if anything.) That is because he is, probably, relatively free of this peculiar notion that physical affection is a finite quantity that can be
cheapened or dissipated—that sleeping with Molly works
some kind of voodoo on sleeping with Susie, or that a
friendly tumble with a casual acquaintance can, according
to some amatory calculus, subtract a googol or two from
one's love for the love of one's life. And accordingly he
is, as Elaine Morgan says, prone to be a little incredulous,
and a little cynical, about all the thinly veiled money talk
with which women mostly attempt to alternately sanctify
and stigmatize what ought to be a fairly simple, ex-
tremely nice fact of life.

"Sex with love," goes the revisionist-uplift line, "is the
crown of creation, compared to which sex without love
is mere physical pleasure, an empty and degrading Brand
X not to be confused with the real top-of-the-line item."
Like most men, I have heard that a hundred times, in so

many words, mostly from women, and never without being reminded of an Irish saying taught to me in my youth: "Sex with love is one of the greatest things on earth. But sex *without* love [pause] is the other one."

Well, they are different, all right, but which is better is a matter of taste and mood and nothing else. The difference is, to simplify, the difference between the predominance of love and the predominance of lust, each of which is a many-splendored thing in its own right. Love needs no advocacy these days, but lust could do with a couple of words on its behalf. As always in the past when the female influence has been in the ascendant, lust has lately had some harsh things said about it, and seems in danger of going, if not out of practice, out of style. Feminists have been saying what women have pretty much always said, at least in public: that it is nasty, brutish, and short, and probably incompatible with their gentle and genteel vision of utopia. What might a man, acting out his own sex's traditional skepticism about such statements, say back in its behalf?

First, as for its notorious brevity: So, he might say, is life. A Sunday School teacher of mine used to tell my class, almost thirty years ago, that lust was brief; now she's dead, but my lust lives on. As for its much-written-about emptiness when unredeemed by love—well, fie. By itself it may be deficient in various fine qualities, but it has its own message, and its own integrity. It's purer. That's the main thing. It is intense, rather than homely; it reaches into the same registers achieved by symphonic music, as opposed to operatic, abstract as opposed to representational art, mathematics as opposed to mechanics.

In fact, to refer to loveless sex as particularly "sensual" is almost the opposite of the truth: It is in the marriage bed, rather, that the creaking springs or the cracker crumbs between the sheets are likely to obtrude in their

176

sensory thinginess rather than as symbols of something vivid. (Creaking springs! What savagery! Cracker crumbs! What nitty-grittiness!) Lust is, or aspires to be, otherworldly, in a sense inhuman, a nostalgic longing for what we were before becoming what we are.

As a result—and just as important—it is funny. It is sometimes alternately, sometimes simultaneously, sublime and ridiculous, the cause of perhaps most of the grotesque and incongruous behavior in any human's life, and therefore a great teacher that things are not the way we're taught they are. To sleep around is to learn, to probe the contours of illusion and disillusion, to prove and re-prove the in a way saddening, in a way reassuring fact that everyone, however godlike at first, is human, is like you. And there is no more important lesson than that.

My friend Neil recalled, once, the moment of truth for him. "I will tell you a major truth," he said. "I will confess something. When all was said and done, what used to turn me on most about fucking was what the guidebooks refer to as the woman's 'response.' You know what I mean. Moaning. Panting. Whooping and shrieking, and thrashing around. The more hullabaloo, the better, was how I felt about it.

"I spent a summer once with a woman named Carol who was simply amazing at that—there are cockroaches who will be deaf for life because of her—and I loved it. One night the air conditioner broke down, and we opened the windows without thinking and then went to it, and when we finished we suddenly heard this cheering and clapping from outside. What seemed like half the tenants on her side of the building were hanging out their windows, giving us an ovation.

"Well, she almost died; she said she'd have to change her name and move, and I don't think either of us left that apartment for about three days, but I told her never to change, and I meant it. After all, why should she? A man, at such times, likes to know that a woman is enjoying herself, and, also, he likes to feel appreciated. I never felt so appreciated in my life as I did during that summer.

"Anyway, all that changed one day when I was having lunch at home and turned on the television. The sound came on before the picture, and the sound was like a hall full of Carols, at full throttle—nothing but shrieking and hooting. Then the picture came on, and it turned out to be a show called 'Let's Make a Deal.' Have you seen that show? It's nothing but this squamous little pustule of an emcee holding out money and pictures of expensive things and promising to positively reinforce the woman who makes the biggest spectacle of herself. And I can tell you, the competition is fierce. Not only do the women all make like an orgy in an echo chamber, but they all dress up as giant turnips or ashtrays or God knows what, which was something that no woman ever did for *me*. I mean to say, it was profoundly disillusioning.

"I could live with the knowledge that there was probably a certain amount of faking going on with old Carol —after all, it was kind of sweet of her, wasn't it?—and it didn't bother me at all to think that she'd probably been in just about the same decibel range with every other boyfriend she'd had. Actually, that was part of what made her the eternal feminine, in my book: I always liked girls who liked sex a lot, because *I* liked sex a lot, and it's good to share enthusiasms, right?

"But this was something else. I was forced to face the fact that as a lover-boy I was, by my own criterion, a good cut below a four-piece living-room set in durable Herculon. I'd never been bothered by the idea that sex turned people into something like animals—animals are nice, most of them—or even into spiritual beings, although that was a good deal harder to take, but I don't like the idea that it turns us into something like shoppers. Which, of course, it does.

"So that was it, or anyway the beginning of it. The dream was over. It became gradually clear to me that, though fucking was still one of the really terrific things on earth, it wasn't interstellar, for women any more than for us. The women I was with after that seemed to pick this up, and the ruckus on the whole was a little subdued, and all in all they seemed to be a little relieved, if anything.

"Like I said before, I'm glad you and me were able to go through that: glad, most of the time, that I got it out of my system, as they say, but also glad that I had it in my system in the first place. Because getting it out—and, I don't mind saying, it certainly took a good deal of getting—was great."

It's true, what Neil says about lust—that is one of the things you learn. In fact, everything is true: the metaphysical poetry and the dirty jokes, even the ho-hums. Even the charge leveled against it by feminists nowadays —that far from being an indecorous return to nature (as their grandmothers used to believe), it represents a dehumanizing abnegation of natural sympathies—can be true at times. Loveless lust can indeed be dehumanizing (the same is true of thinking), and it can be devastatingly cruel (but then so can love). It's not for everyone; and in fact very few of us, probably, are endowed with the capacity to get through half a lifetime without starting to want something else and seeking that separate peace called marriage. Which is just as well, since lust tends to promote satellitic relationships, the moderately attractive many clustering around the magnetic few, with lots of people left out in the cold. A social world monopolized by it would be nastier than our own.

But in its season, there's nothing like it. It teaches you

things nothing else can, one of which is that energy begets energy, that human beings aren't adding machines swapping finite and fungible sums of spirit. It is just absolutely great, in short, and a life lived without indulging in it for a time at least is a poor thing, more diminished than the life of one born color-blind or lame.

Such, anyway, is my view of the matter. That it remains predominantly a *man's* view, despite all the celebrated upheavals of the recent past, is confirmed by the current feminist soul-searching over the propriety of its public representation, and by the deep ambiguities about the sexual revolution which that soul-searching expresses.

Uniquely in the history of censorship, feminists have recently objected to pornography on grounds of what they sense to be its substantive, specifically political, content. They accuse it of being fascistic, a patently absurd charge to anyone who has seen *Deep Throat* or read *Fanny Hill;* insofar as pornography has a political content, it is usually woozily leftist, even Marxist: "Let's all strip off these here trappings of private property and get really communal." Mainly, though, pornography is just a version of pastoral, perhaps the last. It presents an idealized, simplified picture of a messy and immensely important realm of experience that almost all of us have a stake in interpreting to our own ends.

Especially women, according to the old order. That is why feminists, reversing the traditional and much more defensible line against pornography—that it is devoid of substantive commentary and therefore not entitled to protections of free expression—insist, bizarrely, that on the contrary it is suffused with an ideology so odious (here's where the Auschwitz analogies start flooding in) that a country which permits the free circulation of *Mein Kampf, The Communist Manifesto,* and *Against Our Will* still ought to think twice about allowing it in public.

Which analysis has in turn forced feminists into the

even less defensible assertion that pornography is a uniquely male phenomenon—the record of man's insufficiently repressed hatred of women. They have gone into the most spectacular contortions trying to prove that female pornography does not exist; or that anyway, if it does, it's something fundamentally different, sweeter and more humane ("erotica" is the favored word to distinguish them) than male pornography. But the difference always turns out to be one of gentility and coyness—soft focus in Siam instead of klieg lights in the director's bedroom—and as such reflects nothing but the characteristic bourgeois, and feminine, insistence on keeping up appearances.

The difference between pornography and erotica is the difference between being drunk and being inebriated; that is it—there's nothing else. And even then, when one considers the tenor of the work of such women as Pauline Réage, Ayn Rand, Judith Krantz, Grace ("Hurry," she moaned. "Hurry! Hurry!") Metalious, and Jacqueline Susann, in addition to the scores of confession magazines (most of which seem endlessly fascinated with the theme of incestuous rape) being sold monthly to millions of women, it becomes awfully difficult to consider female pornography as being even marginally classier than its male counterpart.

All it is, on the whole, is somewhat more skittish, somewhat more sanctimonious (the bad girls tend to come to bad ends), somewhat more diffuse—in a word, softer. Compared to male pornography, it can be seen as either relatively temperate, if you prefer it, or retarded, if you don't: Its stock-in-trade at the moment is stuff that would have been stopped at Customs twenty years ago, but which the male vanguard has now made to seem fairly tame. In any case, both amount at heart to the same thing: a fantasized escape, sometimes violent, from the burdensome wet-blanket-and-cold-shower role that women have traditionally assumed in the sexual dialectic.

Feminists are, to be sure, correct in one way, and only one, when they say that the cinematic depiction of a man and woman coupling represents a political assault, not on that particular woman or that particular man, nor on all men and women, but uniquely on women as a class. The public representation of an individual's act can be said to reflect on the group of which she is a member to the extent that such a group considers itself a united front, with common interests against a common enemy, and it can be said to threaten that group to the extent that it undermines the way in which, in consultation with those interests, it prefers to have itself represented. The political message of pornography—and this is the one genuine way in which it is indeed a challenge to women as a political entity—is the one delivered at Olympus by Tiresias: that, whatever they say, women like it too; that we men here in the audience see through their ice-maiden routine, and comprehend its mercantile source. It will cease to have political content—and, possibly, start to dwindle away—on the day that the Juno strategy ceases to be in operation.

As of now, that day has, clearly, not yet arrived. Hence the latest continuation of the age-old female campaign, which has been, for reasons of purest self-interest, to play up the consolations of love and impugn the epiphanies of lust. In the past, as now, women have been the prime movers of this campaign, though sometimes acting as the ventriloquists of some Bowdler or Comstock or other soured old man. Whatever their language, their reasoning has been the reasoning of the marketplace, behind which has been the need to convince men of the unique preciousness of something, sex, whose uniqueness is illusory and whose preciousness is mainly a matter of packaging and price-fixing. So we get much angry talk to be filed under "Standards, absence in males of": Doubtless Juno gave Jupiter to understand that he was lowering himself in everyone's eyes by sleeping with mere mortals, and variants of the charge have enlivened domestic hearths ever since.

It is possible to find causes for the disparity in our evolutionary heritage (females of many species customarily withhold themselves from rival males until one has bumped the others off, presumably to improve the pedigree; as for males, male houseflies have been observed attempting to mate with raisins), but it's hardly necessary; we all left the savannah a long time ago. Economics, not genetics, is the field in which our struggles for survival are fought, and the traditional female position makes perfect economic sense.

Monogamy is rooted in supply and demand, and when the balance shifts, so does the sexual ethos. Rigidly Catholic Paraguay, after exterminating most of its young men in the War of the Triple Alliance, adopted a code of promiscuity and (like Athens under similar pressures in the Peloponnesian Wars) legal polygamy, and something of the same cause may well have been behind the first wave of the sexual revolution, following the anthrocide of World War I.

As those examples recall, it has not at all been a story of men always rigging things for their own benefit—unless you believe that the saga of the male sex has been one long chapter in the history of masochism. Women, throughout the past and into the present, have identified their interests and fought for them, tenaciously and effectively, in public and in private. The Millett thesis, that men have run everything and made women into what they are, is not only a prescription for defeatism (if that's really the way it's always been, for a million years, what on earth makes you think it will change just now?) but wildly at odds with the observable facts. "Primitive" or "civilized," it has not been just a man's world, not at all.

6

Founding Mothers

N the last few centuries, the traditional power struggle between the competing interests of men and women has become, like much else, politicized, made over into ideology; what was once worked out in bedroom and village square is now the business of caucus and parliament. But the essential terms of the conflict have remained the same, at least up until roughly the last two decades—and there is plenty of depressing evidence that even in the present age its nature hasn't changed that much, however revolutionary the slogans may have seemed at first. The more one sees of feminism these days, the greater seems its resemblance to its nineteenth-century original, and consequently to the age-old Juno strategy from which that arose. Many influential women, on what level of conscious calculation it is not possible to say, are apparently rediscovering what their grandmothers, and *their* grandmothers before them, knew all about—the political uses of selective purity.

In the Anglo-American cultural tradition, the political stage of the sexual struggle seems to have its origins in the seventeenth century, when for various reasons

the female interest aligned itself with the Puritan amal-
gam of piety and profiteering. From that point, personal
arguments began to be made into sectarian ones, later
to become (under the leadership of that Quakers'
daughter, Susan B. Anthony) political and, in our own
time, ideological. By the end of the seventeenth century, there appears a rough equivalence between female
and Puritan (or roundhead) values on the one hand,
and male and Royalist (or cavalier) values on the other;
and the word "prude" is in the middle of its etymologi-
cal metamorphosis from a word meaning "respectable
woman" to a word meaning "insufferably censorious
Gawdhelpus."

You can find the opposition preserved in the period's
literature, beginning with William Wycherley's 1675
comedy *The Country Wife,* in which a dedicated woman-
izer named Horner, by having himself falsely declared a
eunuch, sees to it that the randiest women in town will,
first, give themselves away (by being the ones most hor-
rified by his presence) and, second, when disabused,
yield to his advances (because their reputations will be
safe). When put to the test, the public protestations of
virtue, by women with names like Lady Fidget and Mrs.
Squeamish, almost always prove hypocritical.

That, as of 1675, is how the sexes square off according
to Wycherley: traditional bourgeois propriety and cant,
against traditional patrician license. The edge of nastiness, of animus and something like thirst for vengeance
that many have sensed in Horner ("Ay, but if he loves
me, why should he ruin me?" asks his most appealing
conquest, and it's a real question), has its origin less in
sex than in antagonism between parties and, behind
them, sensibilities; Horner is as much a scourge as he is
a stud, a muckraker on the trail of a cover-up, and his
Watergate is the female front.

And that, alas, has pretty much been the story since:

Lord B. against Pamela (can anyone these days read *Pamela* without rooting for her abductor? Kate Millett, maybe); Lord Byron against the Bluestockings; generations of fictional ingenues in peasant blouses being rapt away into forbidden regions by Count Dracula in one incarnation or another; the innkeeper's daughter tied to the bedpost, and her renegade horseman, resplendent in lace and silver, riding, riding. Clark Gable and Claudette Colbert do a fine variation on the theme in *It Happened One Night,* in which Gable wisecracks and at one point literally slaps Colbert into realizing that the world is not limited to the smug and upholstered region inside her head. The theme is disguised because the woman is cast as the upper-class party, the man as socially beneath her, but the disguise is thin: The American upper class has always been devoutly bourgeois in its values, and Gable plays a member of the press, that fourth estate conventionally beyond class. (Besides, anyone who has seen the movie—or just about any other Gable movie—can have no doubt about who the real prince is when he's on the screen.)

Feminists will tell you, desperately, that women respond to such stories at least as much as men do as a consequence of the most successful brainwashing campaign in history. The obvious truth is almost the opposite. Women, largely through their own choosing, have taken a stance in relation to men that requires them to be hypocrites, and to know that they are hypocrites. They have allowed themselves to get stuck with the virtue routine. To this day, the streets are full of women working to revive the lingering sense that the presence of a woman is grounds for refraining from laughing at anything really funny; to this day, to force oneself to use the new woman's idiom—"spokesperson," "flight attendant"—is to feel the clammy air of the rectory seeping into one's bones.

The reaction to that sensation has generally been the predictable one—ridicule, debunking, laughter. Henry Fielding, who along with Samuel Richardson epitomizes the difference between eighteenth-century male and female sensibilities in England as neatly as Voltaire and Rousseau do in France, wrote the original male's-view revision of that female fable *Pamela.* He changed the persecuted young innocent to a man, named Joseph Andrews; the randy pursuer to a woman, named Lady Booby; and invited the reader to observe how ridiculous that reversal made the whole thing look.

Along with pornography, humor has always been a predominantly male weapon in the propaganda war, which is one reason feminists are made so uncomfortable by both, and why female pornography cannot be admitted to exist. Both, after all, are forms of escape; and escape (or rescue) from the crystal palace of feminine proprieties is, under the established setup, the definitive male act. That becomes most obvious in the nineteenth century, especially in that Victorian age, named after the woman whose displacement of the regency's wining and wenching with her own famous refusal to be amused represents the high-water mark so far of the female influence, which preceded our own. John Stuart Mill summed it up: "He who has a wife has given hostages to Mrs. Grundy."

In America, the ascendancy of the female influence at this time was if anything even more complete. Feminist cultural historian Ann Douglas has told the whole squalid story in her masterful study *The Feminization of American Culture,* which details how American women of the nineteenth century "exercised an enormously conservative influence on their society": American women, already the readers and writers of most of the books published and the absolute masters of the all-important circulating libraries, joined forces with the clergy to become the source of a flood of morbidly sentimental art and literature (anyone who remembers the relics of Miss Emmeline Grangerford in *Huckleberry Finn* has a fair idea of the type) and the main force behind the public legislation of private morality.

As a feminist, Douglas is obviously uncomfortable with some of the implications of what she shows. She argues that the (in Harriet Beecher Stowe's phrase) "Pink and White Tyranny" of women and clergy resulted from the disenfranchisement of both; that both were more or less forced into their common cause by contemporary pressures: "The minister and the lady were appointed by their society as the champions of sensibility. They were in the position of contestants in a fixed fight: they had agreed to put on a convincing show and to lose. The fakery involved was finally crippling for all concerned."

But at the same time, she is too good a scholar to blink the conclusion to which her findings lead—that the feminine ideal so resented by today's feminists was established, promoted, and enforced by women, as part of a campaign against what they considered the excesses of male lust and male freedom. She tells, for instance, the story of Eliza Farnham, an eastern lady and "publicist for the superiority of women," who, on a tour of the western frontier, is shocked to discover a wife working beside her husband in the fields. Trying to bring the husband subtly around to her own idea of woman's proper elevated place, Farnham asks him coyly "if he is building his new house to protect his 'bird.'" (History, in its ironic way, would have her sisters of the next century declaring that "chick" was a macho put-down, invented by men to keep women in their place.)

Douglas continues:

We the readers are of course supposed to realize that Farnham is referring to the farmer's wife; her little metaphorical flourish is a calculated way both of reminding us of her own literary good breeding and of instructing the farmer with what elegantly euphemistic terms he ought to honor any woman. The westerner, however, insists that he is not sheltering a delicate creature weaker and more sensitive than himself; instead, he crassly compares his wife's physical strength to that of several of his beasts of burden. His clinching line is the edged remark: "I don't know what you Yankees call a 'bird,' but I call her a woman."

Toward the end of her book, Douglas presents a strong case for the proposition that much of the age's memorable literature—all those pilgrims lighting out for the territory, withdrawing into womanless retreats, sailing the seas—can be explained as a reaction against this "Pink and White Tyranny" ("marshmallow gentility," Mencken was to call it later), the cultural rebellion of men against female dominance. Her main example is Herman Melville, who in *Pierre* "presents a savage study of the conspiratorial interaction between genteel religion, feminine morality, and polite literature against the interests of genuine masculinity," and whose greatest book, of course, is all about men doing manly things, with not a woman in sight.

Which, in a way, is where we in the present age come in. "Well," says the narrator of *The Women's Room,* if you don't want to hear about her women friends "you can go read about whales, or stockyards, or rivets if you like. . . ." Obviously, *la lutte continue.* One way of viewing Kate Millett's *Sexual Politics,* which has pretty much set the tone for modern feminism, is as the latest round in that nineteenth-century battle, a counterattack on behalf of the Pink and White brigade whose antagonists have been, in the previous century,

Melville and Twain, among others, and in our own, Millett's targets—Mailer, Miller, and their English ally, Lawrence.

Because Kate Millett and her progeny are, demonstrably, the spiritual descendants of those Bluestockings who in England convinced the despairing Byron that cant was driving out cunt from his native land, and who in America made "the voice of society" a phrase synonymous with pious pap. Amid all the confusions and contradictions of modern feminism, nothing is as clear as this pedigree.

The lineage can be traced in two main stages. First, the feminism that gathered force toward the end of the nineteenth century quite clearly saw itself—and quite accurately, too—as the logical outgrowth of the earlier female campaign to reform the male libido and rein in male liberty. "To bring about the true Christian civilization, which can only improve the condition of our sex, the men must become more like women, and the women more like angels," goes a typical woman's novel of 1854 (quoted by Ann Douglas.) Twenty-five years later, its author had become a feminist orator, and the women's movement, whose slogan was to become "votes for women and purity for men" was under way.

Modern feminists often find it convenient to suggest that nineteenth-century suffragism evolved naturally from the abolitionist cause, but its political alliances were just as pronounced with No-Nothingism, Comstockery, and Prohibition, and in fact it was, for much of its history, overtly racist, as Sheila M. Rothman has recorded in *Woman's Proper Place:*

The first official document of the movement, the Declaration of Sentiments issued at the Seneca Falls Convention of 1848, complained bitterly that women, the guardians of morality, had less political power than vicious immigrants. "He has with-held from her rights," argued the Declaration, "which are given to the most ignorant and degraded men—both natives and foreigners." And this theme became still more important to the agitation in the following decades.

So much so, in fact, that fifty-six years later, Ida Husted Harper, following a strategy laid down by Susan B. An-thony herself, was promoting woman suffrage as an elec-toral antidote to "the foreign vote and the colored vote."

In all other ways as well, turn-of-the-century feminism was what anyone today, even Susan Brownmiller, would recognize as a profoundly reactionary movement. It was, as I have already noted, a decisive force behind the Com-stock Laws and the statutes introduced against birth con-trol and abortion. The Mann Act of 1910—which rests on the assumption that a woman sleeping with a man not married to her is being raped, whatever she may think, because everyone knows that women are immune to mere lust—was one of its proudest legislative achieve-ments.

The same reasoning produced the "purity crusade" against "white slavery," whereby patrons of prostitutes, or male lovers of underage females, were presumed to be the willing beneficiaries of underworld myrmidons in-jecting innocent country women with drugs that made them do shocking things against their will, and the up-shot of which was that a lot of poor horny sods spent a lot of years in jail. (*That* part Susan Brownmiller would approve of.)

As for Prohibition, it was feminism's pet project; a major argument for woman suffrage was that women would forthwith banish John Barleycorn and so elevate the national *ton.* As Peter Gabriel Filene notes in *Him/Her/Self: Sex Roles in Modern America:* "A large propor-tion of the early leaders of the National American

Woman Suffrage Association entered work via the WCTU [Woman's Christian Temperance Union]." (Even today, women favoring a return to Prohibition outnumber men by three to two.) It was, as they say, no coincidence that the Woman Suffrage amendment followed the Prohibition amendment in rapid succession: Prohibition was in fact one of the two major initial accomplishments of the feminist cause, the other being the election of Warren G. Harding. (If you want someone to blame for the American Mafia, which established a foothold with the bootleg traffic of the 1920s, blame women.)

First and foremost, the public enemy at the top of the feminist list was male lust, which was assumed to be the only kind of lust extant. On this score, the evidence is overwhelming, and overwhelmingly depressing. There were a few honorable exceptions—notably Victoria Woodhull, Elizabeth Cady Stanton, and Emma Goldman —but, in the mass, it is safe to say that no other group since the medieval Cathars has been so devoted to the proposition that humanity is redeemable precisely to the extent that it can refrain from sex, or at least refrain from enjoying it. That was in fact one of the points of the Prohibition campaign, as quoted in Sheila Rothman's book:

The sex life is dominated by a compelling instinct as natural as eating and drinking. The laws of custom and modern civilization demand that the sex life be under the control of reason, judgment, and will.

Alcohol makes all natural instincts stronger, and weakens judgment and will, through which control must act. . . .

ALCOHOL INFLAMES THE PASSIONS, thus making the temptation to sex-sin unusually strong.

ALCOHOL DECREASES THE POWER OF CONTROL, thus making the resisting of temptation especially difficult. . . .

AVOID ALL ALCOHOLIC DRINK ABSOLUTELY
The control of sex impulses will then be easy and disease,
dishonor, disgrace and degradation will be avoided.

"Tyrant law and lust reign supreme with him," Susan
B. Anthony had said of man in 1860, urging her charges
to work to reform tyrant lust out of their husband's systems, and that crusade was to remain at the heart of the
feminist platform up until 1920.

A suffragist flyer from 1917, also quoted in Rothman's
book, follows the Anthony logic of fifty-seven years ago
and suggests the extent to which woman suffrage was
envisioned not as expanding freedom but as expanding
the opportunities to curtail it:

A FOOLISH MOTHER loves her children only in the house.
A WISE MOTHER loves her children wherever they go. AN
EFFICIENT MOTHER follows her children out of the house,
into the street, to the school, to the movie, the factory, and
stands between the child and evil influences, low standards,
bad sanitation, disease, and vice. THESE CONDITIONS ARE
CONTROLLED BY VOTES. HOW MUCH DO YOU
LOVE YOUR CHILDREN? Answer by joining the women
who LOVE CHILDREN EVERYWHERE. JOIN THE NEW
YORK WOMAN SUFFRAGE PARTY.

Recalling such language, it becomes easy to understand why George Orwell, writing thirty years later, was
to make the Anti-Sex League, staffed entirely by serious
young women wearing across their midriffs red sashes
that clearly recall the suffragette's distinctive insignia, a
major fixture of *1984.* And if that sounds like a lurid
analogy, listen to the modern feminist Kathleen Barry
describing in *Female Sexual Slavery* the techniques by
which deviants might be brought into line: "When a
particular individual may not be easily moved from being
sexually stimulated by deviant pictures to being sexually

stimulated by nondeviant pictures, olfactory aversion, the introduction of noxious odors with the deviant pictures, may be used. Treatment is considered successful when the individual gets no more than a 20 percent erection to deviant slides."

That, precisely, is how the turn-of-the-century feminist platform sounds when translated into the Newspeak of modern mind-control technology.

I said earlier that modern feminism connected with the heritage of Victorian female piety by way of two major stages. That was the first stage: The first wave of feminism was, on the whole, simply feminine propriety and priggishness, politicized. As for the second stage, Kathleen Barry, along with many, many others, exemplifies it: Much of modern feminism is simply a recrudescence of the purity crusade, the age-old campaign of women against men being allowed to do what they want, be it drinking or whoring or putting on airs.

It is impossible to read through the writings of today's feminists without coming to the conclusion that, for many of them, the central issue is: Men shouldn't be allowed to get away with it, whatever it is.

Some of them openly acknowledge their heritage. I have, for instance, in my casually accumulated files, no fewer than five separate glowing testimonials written by modern feminists to that fist-faced little one-woman goon squad, Carry Nation, the one who made a name for herself by hatcheting men's drinks out of their hands on the grounds that Why weren't they home with their wives where they belonged?, and who was as responsible as anyone for the most catastrophically meddlesome piece of social legislation in our nation's history since slavery.

I have another clipping on Elaine Noble, the self-proclaimed lesbian elected to the Massachusetts legislature (I voted for her, once), who, having been at times the victim of various trashings and threatening phone calls, should presumably be able to appreciate the drawbacks of vigilante justice, and yet who recommended the local feminist Marcia Womangold for a city medal when Ms. Womangold pumped a bullet through the window of a bookstore on the grounds that it sold, among its many other offerings, *Playboy* and *Penthouse.*

I wonder: Why, if these women have really been as repressed as they say they have, are they themselves so enamored of this kind of thuggery? What is it that prevents them from seeing what almost anyone else can see about these people—that the country would probably be a better place today if Carry Nation had been strangled in her cradle, and that Boston would be a safer place if Marcia Womangold were behind bars, where she belongs?

The sad answer, of course, is that they are the soul sisters of such pills, past and present—the direct descendants of the Victorian lady's strategy of using the Bible to beat back the male, thus keeping the lid down and the price up.

Some of the parallels are eerie. Of a female-authored nineteenth-century anthology of temperance fables, Ann Douglas observes in *The Feminization of American Culture:* "Their message is overwhelmingly that man's brutality has no function but the torture of woman," and goes on to cite two exemplary formulae from the same school, "Man the murderer and woman the mourner," "a fiend and an angel." Today we have Susan Brownmiller's definition of man as a raping biped, the representative husband in *The Women's Room* who turns out to be a closet Nazi, and all that Auschwitz imagery.

When Mary Daly declares that semen is a carcinogen and advises women to stay clear of it, she is simply rerunning Christabel Pankhurst's interesting assertion (quoted in Piers Brendon's *Eminent Edwardians*) that "the secretion of the testicles . . . if wrongfully used . . . is so potent that it may figuratively be classed with the secretions of the poison fangs of venomous reptiles."

As for my friend Mira's thoroughly typical insistence that straight thinking is a masculine trap, Filene shows that it was all said before by quoting the suffragette Harriet B. Laidlaw: "Remember, it is more important to be aroused than to be accurate. Apathy is more a crime than exaggeration in dealing with this subject."

A hundred years ago, women reformers were advocating the castration of sex deviants. It is an idea whose time has come back, in the slogan "Disarm rapists."

The Victorian feminist Elizabeth Blackwell urged that military brothels be closed down and that the troops instead be given uplifting lectures and made to work harder. That, plus masturbation, is Susan Brownmiller's plan for our boys today.

In 1891, in what the press called "the war of the righteous women," five hundred society ladies protested the hanging of two nude canvases in the Pennsylvania Academy of Fine Arts; today the righteous women call themselves Women Against Pornography, and they're still at war.

In the previous century, the list of things opposed on principle by women included, to quote David J. Pivar's *Purity Crusade,* "prize fighting, football, the ballet, and nudity in art and photographic reproduction," and Frances Willard urged Harvard and Yale to settle their differences in the debating hall instead of on the football field. Ballet is probably okay nowadays, but otherwise the list is the same, and football is still near the top.

To be sure, feminism was not and is not a monolith—far from it—and in the early years of this century it changed, radically and for the better. Sheila M. Rothman has documented how Jane Addams and her disciples helped reverse the movement's stand against immigrants and minorities. The traditional opposition to birth control was done in by Margaret Sanger and others, who managed to convince enough women that prohibitive legislation hurt them even more than it did men.

As for sex itself, that was the field of the most profound change. The suffragettes had always been aware of the charge that, in promoting sexual equality, they were working to bring about what Robert Briffault called "the perfectly appalling logical consequence that the morals of women shall in future be the same as those of respectable Christian Victorian man—at best," and thus "the total collapse of Christian morality." But they had a ready answer: Women would end the double standard by raising men to their own level. Filene quotes Susan B. Anthony, who, as usual, enunciated the program: "If women would require the same purity in men that men require in women, and if mothers would refuse to entertain in their homes or to give their virtuous daughters to men whom they know to have transgressed the moral code, society would soon undergo a purification—a revolution."

And so the feminist position remained, for a long time. But then came the 1920s. Filene's *Him/Her/Self,* an excellent survey of the period, recounts the change:

Female cigarette smoking jolted the Victorian value structure, but female sexuality smashed it. For many of those who had come of age in that other age, the 1920s were a time of panic and horror. These people included a large number of older feminists, women of [Charlotte Perkins] Gilman's generation, who saw in the flappers a perverse betrayal of their egalitarian hopes. As one mother wrote (anonymously), she had provided her daughter with education, winter sports, symphony concerts, and European galleries, only to discover that the girl had necked with a boy she did not really love, that the girl had "permitted liberties" that were dangerous to self-control, that were vulgar. "Just think," the mother exclaimed bitterly, "in the days of our innocence we all believed that feminism's single standard would be women's not men's."

. . . When older feminists called for an end to the double standard on behalf of chastity, "this new woman only shrugs her shoulders and smiles a slow, penetrating secret smile." She, too, was demanding equality with men, but on men's terms: not only career *and* home, but sexual enjoyment before and during marriage.

This conflict, as well, has been inherited by modern feminism. The difference is that the sequential order has been, if anything, reversed: first the flappers (their short skirts reincarnated in the minis of the late Sixties), then the purity crusade; first Germaine Greer, then Susan Brownmiller. When Adrienne Rich spurns "the false 'liberation' (to smoke cigarettes and sleep around) of the twentieth-century flapper"; when Robin Morgan, going her one better, proclaims that "most of the decently married bedrooms across America are settings for nightly rape" (in the process revealing a wildly inflated notion of the average American husband's libidinal voltage); when Frances Willard, Carry Nation, Josephine Butler, and other such ferrety little prisses are rediscovered and recanonized as feminist saints, it is as if the ghost of Susan B. Anthony, having writhed in agony all through the Twenties, and having perhaps observed with satisfaction that the Depression which followed, and which served us right, was just the sort of thing such activity leads to, had finally returned in force to her rightful place as the sour and flinty heart of what we once called, laughably enough, women's liberation. It seems that George Orwell was right, after all, to give his Anti-Sex League those feminist sashes.

The movement's characteristic imagery has, to be sure, changed in what may seem to be a crucial way. Before, the talk was of men levitating up to women's moral level, and women, if anything, rising to an even uppier up—becoming, in fact, disembodied. Today the talk is often of a kind of neutral, pastoral Alsace-Lorraine between the two sexes.

In many ways, of course, that is a heartening ideal, and from recent evidence more or less achievable: Men and women really have succeeded, over the last twenty years or so, in knocking off many of the old sharp edges, becoming less archetypally provincial and learning to share many more things than they used to. The result has been genuinely liberating. No more having to pretend to like cars and football! No more affectation of ladylike flaccidity, of feet and hands cultivated for the rolled-dough texture of an Ingres odalisque, formed without acknowledgment of floor or work. God, what a relief! The sexes have indeed begun coming together onto a common middle ground, and the process has been almost entirely to the good.

But I would like to register my doubts about whether the same solution is possible for the issue that those nineteenth-century feminist forebears made the center of their program—the conventional discrepancy between male and female lust. Here, the middle ground becomes much harder to imagine, especially if you ask through what adjustments it might be reached. I find it easy enough to accept that most of the old traditional roles were more a matter of social contract than inborn predilection—few people, I would guess, naturally *want* to go forth and get themselves shot, or relish spending their afternoons watching soap operas and washing diapers. Such matters are probably—as in fact they are proving to be—negotiable.

I strongly suspect, however, that lust, or at least male lust, is going to prove a good deal more resistant—that people awaiting the day when it will have been socialized into something compatible with their androgynous visions are going to keep on awaiting, interminably. Frankly, my own reflective recollections of male adolescence suggest to me that a teen-age boy can be raised in a cellar, submitted regularly to sensory-deprivation experiments, kept totally ignorant of skin magazines, TV, Western literature, and any other supposed agent of sex-specific cultural conditioning, and still wind up spending about two-thirds of his waking hours with an erection that *will* not go away, that *will* start up in response to the most outlandish stimuli—a scoop of ice cream, upside down; a piece of purple gauze; an old overheard song.

That is, I suspect that a certain powerful reservoir of sexual feeling is irreducible, certainly for men and almost certainly for women as well, to roughly the same extent. Under the old sexual politics, women were, with considerable strain, intermittently able to disguise or repress their short-term urges in behalf of long-term interests. But there is little chance that men, lacking either precedent or any real motive, would be able to make a similar accommodation, even if they accepted it in principle.

When I ask the students in my "Battle Between the Sexes" class to choose, ideally, between the alternatives of keeping the double standard as is, resolving it by having women adopt men's traditional license, or resolving it by having men adopt women's traditional restraint, invariably the solution they contrive to propose is that the sexes should meet midway, and everybody will be happy.

Well, good luck. My own guess is that this particular golden mean is going down in flames, across the land, approximately a million times a night, to the lilting tune of the gentle but firm female "no." I look around for examples of this new androgynous ideal, and what I see is self-styled adenoidal little sexual beefaloes such as Erich Segal and Barry Manilow. Who are, I'm afraid, an old story, not a new one: just the latest versions of women's men like Samuel Richardson and the Reverend Henry Ward Beecher, feathering their nests by telling the ladies thronged around them what they want to hear: that men can be and ought to be inoffensive little puppies like themselves; that those who aren't are perverse beasts.

I am a certified old-liner who marched against the war and will never buy Saran Wrap as long as I live; but when I contemplate such sorts, I must confess that my heart hungers for another King Gable, another Duke Wayne. Women's men are and always have been, in the eyes of almost all men and probably most women, a thoroughly ignoble lot. Freedom is noble; servitude is wretched; the affected cultivation of servitude is reprehensible. The eagle is luckier than the ox, and both are infinitely superior to the spaniel. By such an instinctive dialectic do most of us, I think, know that the man who gainsays his sex's dower of sexual liberty in exchange for a few gold stars from the local woman's club is a slimy thing, incomparably lower than any standard man or standard woman. Because it always turns out that the price demanded of such a man is palpable, public evidence that his fleshly urges have been canalized into something sweet.

I have been told that in late 1969, David Eisenhower and Julie Nixon were interviewed together about their approaching wedding, that Julie was asked why they were being married in December instead of after their graduation in June, and that she answered in these words, or words to this effect: "Well, of course I wanted to be a June bride, but David just didn't think he could hold out any longer."

All of us who heard this story at the time agreed as one that it constituted grounds for justifiable homicide—or, in this case, femicide. Mr. Eisenhower at that moment faced one of those moral choices that Ernest Hemingway liked to write about—a choice between (1) throttling his affianced on the spot, or (2) accepting his newly proclaimed status as the Wimp of the World, a man who could stand by grinning his idiot grin while the woman beside him bragged to the nation about how she had kept him from ever getting to first base, and here the poor shmuck was going to marry her anyway.

That is an extreme case, but it illustrates neatly what women have traditionally demanded, and continue to demand, of men in return for their public benediction. How is it, for instance, that in spite of a quite serious effort to avoid learning such things, I have somehow picked up the information that that estimable fellow Alan Alda is completely faithful to his wife, that he doesn't fool around with other women?

Although marital fidelity may be a fine thing, the advertising of it is another matter. I'm afraid that the only logical conclusion is that somewhere along the line Mr. Alda saw fit to inform some stranger about a topic on which most of us—quite rightly, I think—were taught to keep silence. At best, it must be that at some point some interviewer—I'll bet it was Barbara Walters—asked him about it, and, in what we can only hope was a temporary failure of will, he held back from giving her the only appropriate answer to such a question: It's none of your business.

Well, that is the price you pay, these days as in the past, for being America's favorite woman's man. Anne Taylor Fleming, in the middle of her published second thoughts about the "postliberation sanctimony" of her fellow feminists, records one example of the kind of thing that gets a man cast beyond the pale:

On the eve of the last Presidential campaign, a woman wrote in The Washington Monthly about the alleged womanizing of Ted Kennedy—behavior, she said, which indicated that he was immature and, therefore, of questionable Presidential caliber. She was not talking about Chappaquiddick. She was talking about casual couplings, "just barely personal and ultimately discardable encounters," which, she said, give "me the creeps."

It was the same venerable reasoning that led a feminist organization in the San Francisco area to oppose Kennedy's candidacy on the grounds that he was widely rumored to be a flagrant exploiter of women, and which, to the south, led Jane Fonda to offer as one reason for voting for her husband instead of then-senator John Tunney the allegation that Senator Tunney was known to go out a good deal with several different pretty young women. (She phrased it less decorously.) It was the logic at work, a couple of years ago, when, in a dinner-table conversation about campus politics, the local feminist leader to whom I was talking rated every male figure discussed according to a fixed standard of monogamous rectitude, and nothing else.

Call it what you will, call it "consciousness-raising" or anything else, what this comes down to is good old-fashioned Grundyism, busybodyism in the literal sense of busying one's mind about what others are doing with their bodies. It was, and is, an important feature of the Juno strategy for keeping men in line, at whatever sacrifice to the enforcers.

"If there were ever a group of people who should be deeply opposed to having people's character judged by what they do or do not do in bed, it is women, so long so judged," argues Ms. Fleming while noticing this strain in contemporary feminism—and that, of course, has always been the best argument for jettisoning it: Setting yourself up as hanky-pank monitor means proclaiming yourself a madonna, and that automatically means that many people suddenly have a vested interest in proving that you're a whore.

It is a high price, but it has been one that women as a group have been willing to pay, and in many cases continue to pay, in return for the leverage it gives them. Whatever it may amount to in other areas of experience, when it comes to sexual conflict, the current androgynous ideal—evoking that idyllic future where everyone is born with Japanesily teeny fingers, the better to work computers with, and nobody except robots has to haul garbage—manifestly comes down to what it came down to a hundred years ago: men behaving the way women want them to, and getting the *yenta* treatment if they don't. What in most areas of experience is a vision of expanding possibilities is in that one crucial area just the opposite—a call for women to retrench and for men to watch themselves, brothers, because the old verities are back in force.

The boundaries separating the ideal from the acceptable man remain what they were, even if he is called a "parenting person" instead of a "gentleman," or an "exploiter" instead of a "bounder." And the campaign against the overt acknowledgment of male lust continues, inevitably, as part of the package, though frequently forced into the most desperate dodges to conceal its source. Look at this article, titled "Erotic Film Festival to Counter *Deep Throat*," from the *Providence Journal Bulletin:*

Waltham Mass. (UPI)—Women students at Brandeis University have come up with a novel way of countering a planned showing of the pornographic movie "Deep Throat" during end-of-semester festivities tomorrow.

They have planned their own erotic film festival.

The university's Women's Coalition says there is a difference between pornography, such as "Deep Throat," and eroticism.

"Pornography is such that it presents society with degrading depictions of women," said Michelle Bowdler, a coalition member. "We wouldn't be opposed to artistic expressions of erotica; erotic films which have a sensual element but don't have violence and sexism."

One of the alternative films is "Orange," described as "a carefully selected point of view of the eating of a naval orange . . . the macro-photography of the soft warm interior of the fruit as it is gently pulled apart creates wonderful erotic sensations."

Michelle *Bowdler!* There are times when life makes things too obvious. A hundred and fifty years ago, Bowdlerism consisted of denying that part of our literary heritage likely to bring a blush to a maiden's cheek; today, it means pretending to be aroused by an orange.

*****

Yes, *la lutte continue.* Forty years ago, the mothers of America banded together to see to it that their boys fighting in the war not be allowed access to anything stronger than 3.2 beer, and successfully thwarted plans to supply them with medically inspected brothels: Their sons might have to die, but that didn't mean they had to enjoy themselves beforehand. Philip Wylie, contemplating the spectacle of a boatload of Gold Star mothers being shipped to Europe to receive congratulations on the sacrifice of their sober, celibate, and dead offspring, coined the term "momism," and opened another front in the battle against the people, female version, whose whole sense of self seems to depend on the enforced and certifiable dullness of other people's lives. In our own time, Susan Brownmiller, taking up the challenge, invites her readers in *Against Our Will* to feel indignant that the U.S. Army could even have contemplated that brothel plan, back then, and blandly offers her alternative to the Vietnam War equivalents:

A regular tour of duty in Vietnam consisted of a one-year stretch, not an unconscionably long period of time to be without a woman, and relief from sexual tension could be, and I presume routinely was, accomplished by masturbation. As one G.I. prisoner of war remarked about his repatriation in February, 1973, "This stuff about not being able to live without sex is nonsense. What I dreamed about was food and medicine."

It is as if, to the Gold Star mothers and Ms. Brownmiller, the fact of war—a male enterprise, by grace of legislation that they seem to stare right through—did not exist, or count. There is no sign here of any sense that a year might indeed be a long time to go without a woman if there's good reason to believe it might be your last year, or that because a hungry and sick man thinks about food and medicine before he thinks about sex does not mean that sex is trivial, unless you assume (as Brownmiller, I think, does) that hunger and illness are trivial, too, when experienced by men.

Such is the cast of mind that can view the past, or for that matter the present, and come to the conclusion that men have always had it their own way—making, in Kate Millett's words again, the "primitive and civilized worlds" into worlds of "male design." A gut-shot nineteen-year-old soldier, according to such perspective, is someone whose ghost can blame his male-bonded brethren for getting him killed and give thanks to his female guardian angels if, at least, he never got drunk and never got laid.

Really, it is hard to imagine a perspective more ungenerous, self-interested, or false. Men do not make women over according to their own design now, and they haven't for a long time, if they ever did. The position of women, as we have inherited it, is the work of her own hands at least as much as those of her consort. Nowhere is this more plain than in the well-documented history of feminism, in which the main enemies of women's efforts for emancipation have always turned out to be other women. (Like the Jewish guards in the camps, goes the rebuttal.) It is true now, and it always was. In *What Women Want,* Gayle Graham Yates quotes a feminist speaker in 1893:

It is often said that the chief obstacle to equal suffrage is the indifference and opposition of women, and that whenever the majority ask for the ballot they will get it.... When Lucy Stone tried to secure for married women the right to their own property, they asked with scorn, "Do you think I would give myself where I would not give my property?" When Elizabeth Blackwell began to study medicine, the women at her boarding house refused to speak to her. ... It is a matter of history with what ridicule and opposition Mary Lyon's first efforts for the education of women were received, not only by the mass of men, but by the mass of women as well.

Filene describes the campaign ten years later:

"I am surprised beyond all things to find how many men are favorable," Harriet Taylor Upton informed a friend while campaigning for suffrage in Ohio. "Now if only stupid women would get awake and yell we might make it." But feminine silence remained smothering. As a fair young belle told one ... organizer in Mississippi, "You know we women do not desire to be other than we are." From a train chugging across the "dead level prairie" of South Dakota, Anna Howard Shaw angrily wrote home to Lucy Anthony that "the women don't want the ballot ... that is true here and no mistake."

It is a matter of record that when feminism did foun-
der, in the Twenties, the cause was a split in the feminist
ranks over whether further freedoms would be worth the
probable sacrifice of traditional privileges. Norman
Mailer, in *The Prisoner of Sex,* remarks on how odd it is
that Kate Millett's account of this century's sexual politics
should entirely skip the Twenties, perhaps the most vola-
tile decade in the social history of the female sex. Well,
this is why: Kate Millett wants us to believe that feminism
was done in by a concerted backlash of Nazis and Stali-
nists and their Anglo-American myrmidons, as cheered
on by Lawrence and Miller.

It is untrue, of course, and any mention of the Twenties in her narrative would make that clear. It was not
Henry Miller (who was banned in America) but the
1923 introduction of the Equal Rights Amendment by
the National Women's Party, and the opposition to it by
such groups as the League of Women Voters and the
Women's Trade Union League, that did the major dam-
age. (The Depression, and then World War II, helped.
But Henry Miller wasn't responsible for them, either.)
Women started wondering what many of them are wondering today: whether the trade-off would be worth it;
whether man's estate, once you got a good close look at
it, was really such a great deal after all. The reason they
have asked themselves that question is that it is a very
good question.

And that growing awareness, of course, according to
one of the most rudimentary tricks of human psychology,
only becomes a reason for turning up the volume even
louder. The feminist reformer Ethel Adamson demonstrated the phenomenon long ago, when her movement's
campaign for a political "sex bloc" collapsed utterly.
"Our theory of the solidarity of women in helping each
other to liberty is wholly fallacious," observed one of her
lieutenants, but Ethel Adamson had the answer: "We

never must be on the *defensive,* but always aggressively *attacking* . . . those women-hating and women-baiting men. . . ."

That has been the strategy in our own age as well, resting on the assumptions that men did everything bad ever done to themselves or to women, and that they should therefore tolerate any abuse heaped on them as a sex. But we didn't. And we shouldn't.

7

Future

SO MUCH for the recriminations over who, in the past, has done what to whom, and who started it. In a way, of course, it doesn't much matter anymore anyway. Whatever the inequities of the past may have been, we live today with a workable consensus that such inequities are no longer tolerable. True, the Nixon Court has recently been edging away from the earlier repudiation of discriminatory legislation—its special cases, so far, have all been to the detriment of men—but there is still good reason for hoping that its skittishness will prove aberrational, a brief turbulence in the current, and that the idea of equality with which this nation began will finally come round, for both sexes, in our lifetimes.

Many of us have already been given glimpses of what the world will be like when that comes to pass. It will, on the whole, be better than it was: Some nice things will be gone for good, but so will a lot of dreck, and what will be gained will outweigh by far the losses. We will all gain a certain measure of integrity and adultness, and lose, perhaps, a certain measure of complacence and style—although Bloomsbury (and this may be a big reason for its vogue) endures in the memory to admonish us that men and women can daily take one another in the round and still be vivid and courtly.

For myself, a famous late-1940s group photograph of literati gathered in New York's Gotham Book Mart to honor Edith and Osbert Sitwell is emblematic of the achievable ideal: There they are, Elizabeth Bishop and Delmore Schwartz and W. H. Auden and Randall Jarrell and Marianne Moore and Gore Vidal and a dozen others, some men and some women, some Americans and some not, some homosexuals and some not, some of them married or lovers, or intermittent or permanent enemies, each of them probably convinced that the superiority of her or his talent to that of everyone else present has not been adequately appreciated, but, for all that, probably also aware at heart that everyone else there is someone to be reckoned with.

Working forward to that state means that we will all continue to undergo what Freud called "education to reality"—reality predictably being more complicated than what we thought—and be made to confront, more than before, the manifold ways in which the inner landscapes of whomever we care for do not necessarily consort with our own ideas of order.

The dialectic of sex is done: good riddance, on the whole. Men, over the last few years, have been discovering, often with some trauma, what that means: that women are increasingly able to look after their own increasingly more sharply defined wishes, becoming in the process less and less charmed by our inherited predilection for taking such matters on ourselves. Welcome, ready or not, to the new world, men: That has been the theme of our recent past.

Those days are now coming to a close, to be followed, almost certainly, by a period in which it is woman's turn to confront the same unsettling message. In fact, for both

sexes the time is approaching when the smug assurance
that things are no longer arranged as our parents thought
will not suffice, when some new and nonfeudal vision of
the sexual order will have to emerge.

As a first step toward that, women will rediscover the
realization reached in time by the first feminist wave—
that the rosy glow around the man's world they are enter-
ing is just about as true to life as the rosy glow around
the hearth and home they are leaving. They will discover, as many are already, that it was, indeed, a good
question that those women of the Twenties and Thirties
paused to ask themselves when they pondered the prospect of losing the protection of discriminatory legislation
in return for the right to meet men on men's own terms.
Did men have such a hot deal after all? After a spell of
soul-searching, the answer most women came up with
was a resounding no.

All the polls and surveys we have, from 1920 to the
present, are unanimous on this point. The consistency—
from Susan B. Anthony's admission in 1902 that most
women did not want the sexual order changed, to the
1970 Gallup poll (the most recent taken) showing that,
by a ratio of three to two, women believe that women
have it easier than men, and the later 1976 Harris poll
showing women rejecting the idea that they are an "oppressed group" by over two to one—is startling. I wonder, is there any other issue about which either sex has
changed its opinion so little for so long? It is all the more
startling considering that, for much of that time, women
have been clamorously urged to think of themselves as
the underdogs, the exploited, the new niggers.

"Brainwashing," has been the inevitable explanation;
but it's been a long time, and sooner or later women will
accept the truth of what feminist Barbara Leon pointed
out seven years ago: "To call a woman brainwashed is a
subtle way of calling her stupid. It implies that we aren't

capable of telling the difference between television screens and real life."

Feminists will start paying attention, as their enemies have for a long time, to the testimony of other women. The fact is that they don't feel particularly oppressed as a sex; if anything, they feel they've maybe gotten the better of the deal. For years feminists have represented women who insist that their lot isn't so bad as either bubble-headed little poopsies incessantly giggling about their clothes or as poor, dragged-out, beaten-down drudges. But they will eventually take a look at some of the women who actually say those things: at Senator Paula Hawkins, for instance, who says flatly that "women already have the upper hand," and who is no fool and no drudge, or at Phyllis Schlafly, who is neither, either.

Making such an acknowledgment would not mean, as Hawkins perhaps and Schlafly for sure would like it to, that women would therefore feel obliged to count their blessings and head gratefully back to the kitchens, with smiles on their faces and smile faces on their aprons. On the contrary: Such an acknowledgment is a necessary condition for the kind of confidence and self-respect that will be required if women are to sustain their brave new freedom as other vogues supplant feminism and the old incantations about female dependency begin coming back in new forms.

To move away from the doctrine that women are and always were nothing but victims to the doctrine that they must be and ought to be protected dependents requires only the subtlest of shifts, as feminism's embarrassing affinities with the New Right keep demonstrating. It is infinitely better, in the long run, to face the perhaps insufficiently melodramatic truth: that women have in the past been pretty much in charge where they chose to be in charge; that they have been about as active as men in the shaping of our inherited world; that a good deal of the credit and a good deal of the blame goes to them; that neither sex is or has been uniquely the victim of the other. The alternative is despair, the consolations of martyrdom, and very little else. Only if it is accepted that women have been able to a great extent to choose their course in the past can it reasonably be expected that they will be able to stick to their new course now.

How has this myth of the oppressed, exploited woman become so firmly rooted? It occurred in the Sixties, when many white upper-middle-class, college-educated women, out of pressures that seemed compelling enough at the time but have long since receded, saw fit to claim for their own benefit the measure of hard-earned sympathy owed to this country's blacks. To this day, this expropriation remains the major obstacle to any effort at working out a noninsane account of the relations between the sexes. From it descends all the canonical utterances about male oppressors and female sex objects, all the efforts to find in any relationship whatsoever involving both males and females evidence of "exploitation."

So a necessary step in redefining realistically the new sexual order is to face, squarely, the truth about this pervasive analogy, which has by now long been obvious: It constitutes an act of such prodigious, Nixonic mendacity that any woman who has gone along with it for a minute would do well to start living with the fact that she has thereby forfeited the right to feel morally superior to anyone else, ever. Did I say a minute? You cannot think about it for thirty seconds without seeing how tacky the whole business is.

Try testing the woman-as-nigger formula, point by point. Has any white woman ever been lynched for abusing or insulting or being suspected of insulting a black man? When do you suppose the last time was that anyone on a sinking ship called out, "Niggers and children first"? At the end of a long list of ways in which women

219

are discriminated against, the feminist Gayle Graham Yates writes: "Finally, women have not been equal to men with respect to the military draft." How does their inequality, which has consisted of being exempted from it, compare with that of black men, which has consisted of being hounded by it? How seriously are you willing to take those studies and novels about the horrors of a housewife's life in the suburban ghetto when you pause to recall what life is like in the real ghetto? How much sympathy do you have left to expend on those Victorian ladies locked in their gilded cages, after you've paused to remember that their black contemporaries were locked in shanties when they were not being whipped in the fields? There are, approximately, eight times as many white women in this country as there are black men; which group, at a guess, do you suppose has occupied the greater number of places of honor for the nation's gas chambers, gallows, firing squads, and electric chairs?

This could go on forever, but enough. It is grotesque. It is insane. There must have been some stupidity potion circulating in the nation's water supply the day such an equation first came to be seriously entertained. There has never been any basis for comparing woman's lot to that of an enslaved or oppressed people—not in ancient history (the average Roman household slave was a man, taking orders from a woman), not in recent history (for every Simon Legree there was a Samantha, and the turn-of-the-century feminists, as I have mentioned, showed no compunctions at all about riding the antiemancipation backlash), and certainly not in the present, when white women have, in their own feminine way, participated quite as enthusiastically as men in the subjugation of black women and men.

As for black women, Mary Ellman notes in *Thinking About Women*, "The novelist Paule Marshall has pointed out, Negro women in America have previously been classified, according to age and figure, as nymphomaniacs or mammies. (White men made use of the first, white women of the second.)"

And as for black men—it was not solely out of their own fevered crania that southern white males cooked up the idea that white southern females were to have their purity protected with rope and fire.

The 1931 Scottsboro trial, at which nine black men were condemned to death on the testimony of two white women, Ruby Bates and Victoria Price, was for a long time the most famous example of woman's complicity in the arrangement, which is why Susan Brownmiller in *Against Our Will* feels compelled to turn intuitive in her handling of the case: "The singular opportunity afforded Price and Bates should be appreciated by every woman. From languishing in a jail cell as the lowest of the low, vagrant women who stole rides on freight cars, it was a short step to the witness stand where dignity of a sort could be reclaimed by charging that they had been pathetic, innocent victims of rape."

Although the facts of the case are now in dispute, it is clear that Susan Brownmiller believes that the women perjured themselves and that the men were innocent— and sides with the women anyway. This is the kind of thing that, when I was living in Cambridge and surrounded by it, moved me to pronouncing the "i" in "ideology" as a short rather than a long vowel, so as to suggest "idiot" rather than "idea." What is "idiology," so pronounced? It is the mental process by which someone who believes that two women for their own advantage have conspired to effect the murder of nine innocent men still manages to give her sympathy to the women. I learned that definition from my conversations with the feminists who used to hang around Harvard Square— including some of the originals of *The Women's Room*— and I would like to say, as one who knows, that there is no purer instance of the form than what feminists in general and Susan Brownmiller in particular produce when trying to work out some presentable policy on the question of the black male.

The trick, you see, is to loudly sympathize with the black male as a fellow victim, in order to drain off for your own profit as many guilt-points from the association as possible, while at the same time withholding any whisper of assent from the notion that the crime of rape, in which the black male exceeds his white counterpart by a ratio of five to one, might be a product of social degradation as severe as that afflicting almost any white woman —might be anything, in fact, but a manifestation of the patriarchal power elite. The trick, that is, is to be both Ramsey Clark (when it comes to American racism) and George Wallace (when it comes to one of its consequences), on the same issue.

Impossible, you may say. Aha, I say back, you obviously haven't (lucky you) read *Against Our Will,* then. Because that is exactly the trick that Ms. Brownmiller, with her Laocoonian twistings and her Henry Mooreian lacunae, with her jumpings through hoops and her selective occultations, manages to pull off.

I would like to pause here for a spell, before moving on. Because we are now approaching what may well be *the* nexus of feminist bad faith. *Against Our Will,* which along with *Sexual Politics* is probably one of the two sacred texts of what is called "radical feminism," is probably as malignantly fraudulent a piece of writing as has been produced in this century. I am not being hyper-bolic: I have read *Against Our Will,* and I have read *Mein Kampf,* and my sober judgment is that it is a toss-up between them. It is virtually not possible to read a page of Ms. Brownmiller's book without coming across some lie, distortion, or fatuity, every single one of them tend-ing to the conclusion that, in the words of Marilyn French, women are great and men are rotten.

You may say that in comparing these two books I am getting a mite overwrought, especially considering how fastidious I have been so far about the feminist penchant for Nazi analogies. Well, I admit it. I am not a Jew, and I am a male, and it may well be that I have been swayed accordingly. No men, after all, have as far as I know yet been exterminated according to any program inspired by Ms. Brownmiller's tract, although a few women *have* gotten away with murdering men.

On the other hand, there remains the fact that Justice Rehnquist, in his decision that the rights of men not to be selectively shot or imprisoned were a matter of mere Constitutional punctilio, was almost certainly not being influenced by the thought of the late Mr. Hitler, and probably was being influenced, not by Brownmiller her-self—even I have a higher opinion of him than that—but by the climate of opinion that she embodies. The French Army, the saying goes, is always ready to fight the last war; I am beginning to feel that the feminists, in their incessant campaign against the Nazis of forty years ago, may be either consciously or unconsciously deflecting our attention from the real enemy of the moment, which is awfully close to themselves.

In any case: Let us take Susan Brownmiller's handling of the subject of white men lynching black males on the testimony of white women. With this subject, we are at the ganglion of feminism's claim—implicit since it coined "sexism" by analogy with "racism"—to have a lock on a certain brand of indignation.

In 1955, in the small town of Money, Mississippi, a fourteen-year-old black boy named Emmett Till, acting on a dare, asked a white girl named Carolyn Bryant for a date. She chased him away with a revolver, and he retaliated by whistling at her before running off with his friends. She retaliated in turn by telling her husband, Roy Bryant, about the incident, whereupon he, with another young white man named J. W. Millam, beat up, mutilated, and killed Emmett Till, and dumped his body in a river. About these facts there is no dispute; their main source is the testimony of the two white men, who were nonetheless found not guilty by a local jury after an hour's deliberation.

How do you suppose one might go about presenting this incident according to the canons of orthodox feminism—viz., that we must be made to pity the pistol-packing woman rather than the murdered fourteen-year-old? It is a challenge, all right, but Susan Brownmiller is up to it. She has three ways.

The first is simple: Her account simply withholds the fact that Carolyn Bryant incited the killing by going to her husband and telling him of the whistle.

Second, she engages in one of those acts of selective sympathy so characteristic of the form—she asks us to try to suspend our normal reaction, to try to see things from Carolyn Bryant's point of view:

And what of the wolf whistle, Till's "gesture of adolescent bravado"? We are rightly aghast that a whistle could be cause for murder but we must also accept that Emmett Till and J.W. Millam shared something in common. *They both understood* that the whistle was no small tweet of hubba-hubba or melodious approval for a well-turned ankle. Given the deteriorated situation—she with a pistol in her hand, he scampering back to safety with his buddies—it was a deliberate insult just short of physical assault, a last reminder to Carolyn Bryant that this black boy, Till, had in mind to possess her.

"Just short of physical assault"—that is, *almost* a rape.

Third, she leads us to understand that she knows how

we feel; that she herself once felt the bleeding-heart liberal's knee-jerk of revulsion to Till's murder, but that she
has now come to see the error of her ways; and that if
we're as tough-minded as she is, we will, too:

It took fifteen years for me to resolve these questions in my
own mind, and to understand the insult implicit in Emmett
Till's whistle, the depersonalized challenge of "I can have
you" with or without the racial aspect. Today a sexual remark
on the street causes within me a fleeting but murderous rage.

The word "murderous," at the end of an attempt to
make us lose sympathy with the victim of a murder, is not
idly chosen. A whistle is *almost* a rape, and murder is a
no doubt extreme but perfectly understandable reaction
to rape—*almost* the right response. That fourteen-year-
old whistler may have been treated a bit rough—but,
hell, he asked for it, and, anyway, you can bet he'll never
try pulling *that* again. It is, all in all, an instructive instance of just what consciousness-raising means when it
comes to race and sex: the process by which a 1970s New
York radical comes by degrees to share the consciousness
of a 1950s Mississippi lyncher, all the while clutching her
leftist credentials: both Ramsey Clark and George Wallace, just like I said.

There is, I should mention, one other way in which
Susan Brownmiller endeavors to make us see that Emmett Till shouldn't get any of our sympathy. She links
him to Eldridge Cleaver: both black, after all; both *male,*
after all; one a professional, self-proclaimed rapist; the
other a professional, unrepentant . . . well, whistler—but
pretty sure to go on to even worse, if he hadn't been
taught that lesson so early.

Poor Emmett Till. Even his killers let him alone after
they'd done with him; it did not occur to them to make
an example of him twenty years later. And poor Ameri-

can blacks. They don't even get to keep their one dubious inheritance of any political value: the sense in some white hearts that blacks are perhaps entitled to a little special consideration. No, some New York hustlers, like a street punk springing tenement mailboxes on welfare-check day or a shyster Fed negotiating an Indian tribe out of the reservation where they've just discovered bauxite deposits, just have got to have that, too.

I confess I am mystified as to why they've put up with it, why they haven't by now loudly repudiated the feminist attempt to expropriate their moral claim on America for the scaly scam it is. I suppose they must have hoped that the alliance would make them more visible to the middle class and so increase their influence. Anyway, they ought to have realized their mistake by now: It turns out the deal is for them to stay in the slums while women —mostly white women—are out cashing the checks on their three-hundred-year deposit of grief. Poor American blacks: taken, again.

That Susan Brownmiller and the women in her camp have gotten away with such a hoax for so long indicates how deep the vein of chivalry still runs in us. We still, men as well as women, want to believe that woman is a creature who goes not on the ground; that if an individual woman is only so-so at this or that, it must be because something really bad is impeding her. And we still resist the testimony, consistent ever since it was first solicited, that on the whole a woman's lot is just about as bad as, and just about as good as, a man's.

So we have been swallowing, and are still swallowing, what the movement's theoreticians call the "black analogy." The formula was, I believe, first popularized by Gloria Steinem—that man to woman equals massa to slave; that the suffragettes equal the abolitionists; that the ERA is a belated Fourteenth Amendment; and that "Sisterhood is powerful" is the "black power" of half the human race. And, as an inevitable result, we have gotten lots of talk about men and women as oppressor and op-pressed, arranged hierarchically, and nothing whatever in the tradition of Plato's comparison of male and female to two halves of a severed sphere, or the Renaissance commonplace comparing them to two partners in a dance, or Lawrence's metaphor of the two suns of a double star. Any hint of any kind of roughly equal trade-off or balance between the two sexes is dismissed in one of two ways: It is ignored, or it is finessed.

The name for the first reaction is, brazenly enough, The Pro-Woman Line, a feminist formula which signifies that its advocates do not wish to quibble about consist-ency, are not going to worry about whether they're being fair (or, as they would say, "fair") or not: They are a union, a phalanx, a swarm, a force of nature, a hungry unicellular protoplasmic globule extending its pseudo-pods whither it can and absorbing whatever it can grasp and hold. The prevailing attitude is that of the Cook County ward heeler: We're looking out for ourselves, and if you don't think it's fair, tough—why aren't you looking out for *your*selves? (A very good question, inci-dentally, men.)

The second strategy, followed by those who want to maintain the illusion that there's some justice in the world and that their side is for it, consists simply of exaggerating all traditional male privileges and female burdens, and belittling all traditional female privileges and male burdens.

Have men, throughout the last several hundred years, been killed off in greater numbers than women because they have selectively been exposed to more hazardous endeavors and environments? The only mention of the fact that you'll find in the feminist press concerns how rough that made life for the single women who had to contend with an unfavorable ratio in the marriage market.

Have men been drafted and sent off to war while women stayed home seeing to it that their boys weren't drinking too much or screwing too much? Well, says Susan Brownmiller, that's because men like war ("War provides men with the perfect psychological backdrop to give vent to their contempt for women"). And besides, adds a character of Joanna Russ's *The Female Man,* it's our natural habitat ("As moths to the flame, so men to the social patterns of the Army, that womanless world haunted by the ghosts of millions of dead women. . . ."). And what's more, continues Kathleen Barry, it teaches us useful "survival skills" denied to women. And anyway, adds Ashley Montagu, we wouldn't have let ourselves get stuck with the fighting in the first place if we weren't just naturally stupider than the women, if we didn't suffer from "underdeveloped imagination" in such matters as what it's like to have one's head blown off.

Marilyn French delivers the *coup de grace:* "Pregnancy is the greatest training, disciplining device in the human experience. Compared to it, army discipline that attempts to humble the individual, get him into the impersonal line that can function like a machine, is soft." You think the Tomb of the Unknown Soldier is a moving memorial? Save your tears for the Womb of the Unknown Mother.

So much for any sympathy for the boys at the front. As for the men back home—well! Just think of them, the lucky swine, getting to do all that meaningful *work* out there in the world while women are left at home to stare at the tube and talk to babies. That's not the way it is anymore, of course, but that *is* the way it was, and women are still trying to get over it.

Just think of how it was a hundred years ago, when the

average Victorian woman got stuck at home with the cooking and cleaning and kids while her husband, just because he was a man, got to dash out and dig that ditch, sweep that crossing, wallop that donkey—or, if he wore a white collar, sit perched high on his clerk's stool copying over all kinds of exciting names and numbers from one ledger into another. Suppose he was one of that small fraction of men—the ones we hear about most of the time in feminist writings—who had some real power and made some real money? In that case his wife's lot was even worse: She didn't have any work to do at *all.* "You do not know what life means when all the difficulties are removed," writes one of Peter Filene's exemplary Victorian ladies. "I am simply smothered and sickened with advantages. It is like eating a sweet dessert the first thing in the morning." Not to mention the servant problem.

Of course, that is not the whole story. There were women (about one in five, up until the turn of the century) who were forced to work out in the world, and—no fooling, now—their lives were terrible. Wanda Neff, in *Victorian Working Women,* details the ways in which they were abused and (for once the word means something) exploited, and she is especially horrifying on the subject of a representative "drawer"—a young woman whose job it was to haul carloads of coal from the mine face to the entrance. It was, clearly, unspeakably degrading.

But it was degrading for the men, too, who were not drawing coal but digging it, because, rightly or wrongly, Parliament in 1842 declared that digging coal was especially strenuous, dirty, and dangerous work, and restricted it to men. Wretched as she was, that Victorian drawer was, rightly or wrongly, generally agreed to have it easier than her male coworkers. (We are more humane about such things today, and the female drawers are long gone. But the men are still down there in the mines.)

And rightly or wrongly, enough of the granddaughters of those patriarchal Victorian MPs felt strongly enough about preserving such protective laws that they were, in the 1920s, willing to split and scuttle the feminist movement of the day rather than see them abolished.

Feminists have a word for people who bring up things like this—for men who try to suggest, as a precocious American male of the 1920s recorded by Filene remarked, that "man's superiority, once it is brought into the light of day and examined, appears to be a liability rather than the asset it has been considered heretofore." The word is "whining." Women protest; men *whine.* The message to men should be clear: Don't go expecting any sympathy when you try to talk these things over; sympathy is a big wide boulevard with a lot of men on one end and a lot of women distributed in a traffic circle on the other, featuring a big yellow sign pointing to the latter reading ONE WAY. Periodically, some movement leaders used to say that women's liberation would free men as well as women from their restrictive roles, and that this would be a good thing—but you can't believe that and at the same time embrace the white master/- black slave analogy (let alone the Nazi/Jew analogy) which has carried the day.

An essential step in trying to get some reasonably accurate perception of the relation between the sexes is therefore to ignore most feminist rhetoric. You must recognize that women organized into a group are pretty much like any other lot organized into a group, be it morticians or baseball players or the National Association of Manufacturers: They will interpret reality in the way that best promotes their interests, to the extent they are allowed to do so. Which means that the next step is to do a certain amount of forgetting: Forget all that woman-is-the-nigger-of-the-world talk. Because it isn't true: You know it, I know it, and even most feminists know it; they just keep using it because it works, and because not enough people have blown the whistle yet.

Then comes the third step, which is finding something better, some way of looking at men and women, and how they relate, that is closer to the facts of life. That's the hard part.

We can begin with a simple observation: Men, on the whole, want to make women happy. That is so obvious a truth that I feel self-conscious saying it, and feel compelled to run my eye over the feminist bookshelf above my head to justify putting it on paper. (Yes, those books are real. Yes, their authors really don't know this obvious truth.) In particular, husbands, for the most part, want to make their wives happy. They may be insensitive or stupid or wrong in trying to figure out how to achieve that, and ineffectual in bringing it about, but it is definitely what they want; it may, in fact, be *the* thing they want.

In nature, the care and gratification of his mate is often a male's *raison d'être,* and there have long been enough reasons for the disgruntled man to think that the same is true among humans. Even the most primitivist analysis of human behavior between the sexes—according to which men see women as breeding machines and women see men as bacon-getters—leads to something like that, since happy breeders have long been presumed to produce the highest-quality babies. It might be a crass and somewhat silly way of looking at things, but a lot less crass and silly than the oppressor-and-oppressed routine.

The fact is, a good deal of traditional female behavior can be explained as an effort to avoid calling up visions of that state of nature, in which males are largely hyperactive dopes bumbling through their suicidal courses for the amusement and benefit of females. To encourage such visions would have been to encourage men—the smarter ones, anyway—to opt out of the arrangement. Working-class women, who know through their husbands how thoroughly uncharming most jobs out there really are, have long understood this very well, which is why they have to a great extent resisted the efforts of their swankier sisters to get the rules changed.

As for the contractual decision that women should be housewives and mothers, that was reached by men and women both, on the testimony, largely, of women, who let it be known that it would make them, on the whole, happy. And it was not, under the circumstances, a dumb move at all, considering the average (male) alternative. The deal was that women would grant to the man a certain amount of largely illusory freedom in exchange for a certain amount of perhaps illusory security, and that each sex would find fulfillment in its own field of, respectively, work and children—gratification that we moderns, being sharp post-Marx folk, have come to think was also illusory.

There was, of course, a good deal of dereliction of various kinds—adulteries and abandonments and beatings and deceptions—and probably men were guilty of the majority of it, it being pretty predictable that freedom will be abused in proportion to its allotment, but that was the deal, as worked out between both sexes; it was what women wanted, and when they started wanting a change, they got that, too.

All this exposition of the obvious is just to suggest that there is a perfectly respectable and time-tested way of looking at the relation between the sexes—crude and often false to the facts of this life or that, no doubt, but on the whole more satisfactory than any other, and much closer to the truth than any we've been getting lately. It is that they have been balanced, as on a scale, each sex with its own particular burdens and benefits, the trade-off between them having been worked out over the centuries so that the apportionment to each is roughly even.

The late Roland Barthes, in an influential essay, revealed the image of scales to be *the* ruling metaphor of bourgeois thought; and feminist theoreticians, following his lead, will be quick to tell you that such talk is just "separate sphere" propaganda, analogous to racist fables about the happy, rhythmic life of simpleminded black folk. Such talk is wholly mythical, they will say; there are no scales in our lives, no trade-offs, and precious little justice, only oppression.

There are indeed no scales in our lives, but there are no chains, either (except in certain pornography and certain feminist tracts), and no legally sanctioned rape (except in the fevered imagination of Susan Brownmiller and her disciples), and no pyramids or iron fists or hobnailed boots crushing downtrodden female masses. There is life, and there are different provisional, inadequate metaphors for describing it, and over the years the metaphors for the relation between men and women that have worn best have included the idea of some kind of equilibrium.

The *locus classicus* in Aristophanes' speech in the *Symposium,* in which men and women are described as the traumatically bifurcated halves of a once perfect being, intermittently trying to recapture their lost wholeness through sexual union. Two thousand years later, one of Castiglione's courtiers, in the midst of some elegant badinage over which sex is superior, updates the idea: The ideal, he argues, is neither sex by itself but both together, forming the "composite which preserves the human species" and approximates androgynous divinity. In our century, the most influential conductor of this image has probably been Jung, with his theory of the male animus buried in every female, and female anima in every male.

To mention such *male* writers (it could have been worse; I could have brought in Lawrence) with anything other than scorn, to suggest that they may have been on to something with such talk, is automatically to invite hoots from the gallery, of the sort that a Nelson Eddy movie, say, is likely to elicit from a college audience. The last age's metaphors always seem at least as quaint as last year's newspaper, and so it is only natural that people can laugh at talk of balances and dances as absurdly dated figures of speech and then head back to their dormitories talking soberly about oppression and exploitation. We are just going to have to wait until they realize that Engels was a mythmaker, too, and by now a pretty antiquated one.

It will happen. Life between men and women is too palpably not the way he said it was for it not to happen. There are two main ways to look at that relationship—as a hierarchy and as an equilibrium—and the latter is certainly going to return, soon. First, because it's due. Second, because it's truer.

The former version—of the sexes as classes, one atop the other—introduced in our age by Friedrich Engels and resurrected lately by way of the radical chic of the Sixties, derived in the first place from a false analogy between men and women on one hand and a "Darwinian" reading of nature (kill or be killed, prey and predator, all that) on the other. Aside from the folly of looking to anything in the wild as a guide to anything in human affairs, the analogy was hopelessly dependent on the realities of early industrial England. Because however things may once have been in Manchester, nature by itself is a lot more than just red in tooth and claw; it is full of examples of happy symbiosis, and there is good reason to think that sex itself is one such example. Sex, writes Fred Hapgood, in his excellent book *Why Males Exist,* is "a social adaptation," a form of "specialization and individuation": The primordial organisms from which we descend separated into male and female for the same reason that their bodies developed right hands and left hands, because it increased the range and competence of the species.

In any case, that has traditionally been the way the two sexes have been represented in relation to one another: side by side, hand in hand, one in the office, the other in the home, neither one on top for good. There have of course been efforts, often successful for a time, to impose on that relation notions of precedence drawn from the social hierarchy, be it feudal or industrial (feminism is the latest such effort), but in the long run they tend, happily enough, to be undermined by the equilibrium's reassertion of itself.

This, in fact, may be the oldest story in the annals of sexual politics. The masculine pantheon of Olympian gods displaces the earth mothers and is in turn countered with the female cults of Dionysius and the Eleusinian mysteries; medieval Christianity's patriarchal condemnation of Eve as the cause of mankind's fall produces the cult of Mary, the second Eve who effectively replaces Jesus as the main agent of mankind's salvation; in the same period, the cult of the untouchably superior lady takes command of the European imagination, and brings with it, predictably enough, the golden age in the literature of antifeminism.

There seems, in short, to be a rooted human tendency to resist the exaltation of either sex at the expense of the other. Human resourcefulness has just been too much for the sexual dogmatists. Male or female, they have yet to concoct a myth of sexual precedence that cannot be made to cut both ways. For every priest or witch doctor telling you that menstrual blood is special, it's cursed, there is another ready to tell you that menstrual blood is special, it's sacred. Does "Genesis" record that man came first, that woman was made from his rib? Well, fine—that can mean that woman is secondhand, derivative, an inferior version of the real thing, or it can mean just the opposite:

> Auld Nature swears, the lovely dears
> Her noblest work she classes, O:
> Her prentice han' she tried on man,
> An' then she made the lasses, O.

So Robert Burns, echoing the same sentiment expressed by Dryden, Pope, and Steele—and, beyond them, stretching back to antiquity and extending up to the present conviction, shared by Kate Millett and George Gilder, that manual labor is best left to the drossy, underrefined, more primal and primitive male.

As for the opposite version, currently being promoted, that women came first—well, fine again: You can read all about it in creation myths about the male *logos* struggling to impose order on the female realm of chaos and old night; let women take what heart they can from *that* story.

For some time I accepted the feminist belief about ancient theories of reproduction and the roles each sex plays in it—I accepted that the doctrine that man deposits the homunculus fully formed in the woman, who acts only as its receptacle and incubator, was a terrible chauvinist distortion that had the effect of reducing woman to nothing. Then one day, in a spasm of that Fauntleroyian feminism to which other members of my sex are still lamentably susceptible, I mentioned to the woman lying beside me in bed how terrible, in my enlightened opinion, it must have been for a woman to think that about her own children. At which point she set me straight.

"Oh, I don't know," she said. "I think it must have been something for a woman in those days to think, when a man shot that little guy into her, that it meant"—and

236

here her fingers curled shut in a gesture the remembrance of which still gives me shivers—"that she'd finally really *got* him."

And I'll bet she was right, too—righter, anyway, than I had been, parroting the piety of the hour.

So any of the prominent myths can be made to work either way, and the two ways tend to balance out. Even today, despite massive propaganda to consider it as some kind of outmoded neoclassical conceit, the image of the balance persists, in disguised form: Our vision of the ideal androgyny really amounts to everyone moving toward the fulcrum and staying there; our idea of liberation more often than not amounts to role reversal—jumping from one arm of the balance to the other. Nothing illustrates this so clearly as feminism's rhetoric, which has almost always been in what Mary Ellman has called the "authoritative mode" typical of masculine writing. "She has," writes Norman Mailer of Kate Millett, "a mind like a flatiron, which is to say a totally masculine mind." It's true, according to the traditional standards—no curves or nuances in Ms. Millett's prose, no sirree—as it is true that Mailer's *Prisoner of Sex* is transparently the work of a man trying to write like a woman.

So even among these sexual revolutionaries, the Aristophanes myth holds: each sex longing on one level to possess, to in a way become, that which on another level it has to consider alien if it wishes to keep its identity. Joyce in *Finnegans Wake* called it "paradox lust," and it is a paradox, in the long run an irresolvable one—this crazy setup whereby X desires to consort with Y to the exact extent that Y possesses attributes that X would be insulted to be considered possessing himself or herself.

At the heart of heterosexuality is its own annihilation, which is why, I think, our classic male and female symbols—John Wayne and Greta Garbo, for instance—tend to be ideally chaste. The old term "lady's man," which denotes an actively heterosexual male and connotes effeminacy, preserves the contradiction. Men and women have wanted one another to be different, so that each could have something to escape to; each has ironically built its own world on the premise of another, foreign sphere of attractions and repulsions—which may be heavenly and may be hellish in the imagination of each, but which in any case performs the absolutely essential function of being otherworldly. We have conned each other, for our mutual good. Many linguists think that the division of reality into polarized opposites is *the* fundamental act of the human brain, and it may be that the heritage of human sexuality is its ultimate creation—two great simultaneously magnetized and repellent principles, coming together in romantic combustions or poised against one another in the equilibrium of civil community.

Other ages have had their own images of how the balance was to be distributed and maintained; our own is conspicuously androgynous, in one of two main versions—either the (once fashionable, now not) Chinese model, in which everyone becomes as unisexually identical as possible, and libido, liberty, and all assertions of individual will that are likely to disrupt the mean are rigorously suppressed; or the "transactional" model, in which most sexual identities are assumed to be electable roles negotiated in relation to one another, and individuals are free to range widely over the traditional repertoire of possibilities—women can be bosses, men can be househusbands—in a kind of social Brownian movement that, following an inner logic similar to that of the marketplace, will seek out its own equilibrium. This latter ideal was the one to emerge over the last decade, and I for one fervently hope that it flourishes in the future.

Although it may be bourgeois, and inadequate in any number of ways, that idea of the balance has a way of reasserting itself, against whatever odds. That, for the most part, is the way we want it to be—in a word, fair. The world may indeed be a history of dogs eating dogs —whether in the form of saber-toothed tigers pouncing on woolly mammoths or of nations conquering nations— but despite intermittent attempts to make that ugly fact apply to the connection between men and women, it doesn't.

The recognition of this truth would work wonders in the current acrimonious sexual dialogue. And all it would take, really, would be for men to listen, seriously, to what's being said, to pay these women the compliment of believing that what they're saying has some meaning according to its relationship to the observable world and that it is therefore capable of being demonstrably more or less right or wrong.

What will happen when we all really take the equality talk seriously, and stop making allowances?

Well, first of all, all the obvious good things that we have lately been encouraged to envision: Women will be proportionately freer to develop their potentials, men proportionately freer from the obligation to prove theirs. Certain species of chronic brutishness and bitchery will recede from the scene. Work, whether in the "real world" or the home, will finally be seen for what it always has been, mostly—a very mixed blessing or a sustaining burden, according to one's temperament and luck. The idle and the harried will cease to envy and glamorize one another's lot. It will perhaps be too much to expect the grosser forms of pornography and prostitution to go away, or to expect the sanctimonious to stop howling about them and mind their own business—there will always be losers, and they will always find one another out—but at least most men and women will come to realize that none of that sad story has anything important to do with themselves. For a few privileged sorts, it will all seem marginally grayer and less electric than in the old days, but the great majority will become freer, more grown up, and happier. Things, in short, will get better.

They will also improve in other ways not so commonly foreseen at the moment, some of them trivial and some of them not.

Trivial: People will feel free to suggest to feminists who wish to show their equality with men by refusing to shave their legs that they also follow the male example of covering up the unsightly result with long pants and thick socks. Fran Lebowitz's recommendation that "women who insist upon having the same options as men would do well to consider the option of being the strong, silent type" will be taken seriously. It will be possible for a man to hold a door open for a woman, or for a woman to hold a door open for a man, without either feeling like soldiers in some ideological campaign; and the current ridiculous Alphonse-and-Gastoning, which the traditional rules of precedence were largely designed to avoid, will vanish.

More grandly, the current process of cultural accommodation to female justices, legislators, and bosses will continue to its logical fifty-fifty conclusion. The time when a woman's accession to high authority was big news is already, happily, mostly past. And, of course, the old preserves of female privilege must wither away in the process, or be pushed. The latest Department of Labor figures show that from 1959 to 1974, when women were pressing for access to white-collar jobs and winning it, their (always very small) representation in the manual-labor force in fact declined further. That will start to change: The female hardhat or coal miner will cease to be what they largely are now, *Ms.* magazine tokens, and women will have some very direct experience of what the men who make the country's grubby machinery work have been going through all these years.

There will, above all, be no question of whether to draft women; they will as a matter of course be drafted right alongside men, and trained, in the same proportion as men, for combat. In the event of war—which, what with the current crew in charge, seems likely—they will be sent into battle to be bloodied and brutalized, just like men, and if the cemeteries and casualty wards don't fill up with women as fast as they do with men, men will be just as justified as black soldiers were during Vietnam in demanding an explanation. I don't mean to be bloodthirsty, but that has got to be rule number one in the new deal, because there is no human right more important than the right not to be killed.

There is a story of a society lady meeting an Edwardian dandy during World War I and demanding to know why he wasn't with the boys fighting in France, to which he is reported to have replied, "Madame, I am the civilization which they are dying to defend." A good story, but of course outrageous, terribly callous and elitist and all. We are finally in a position to know what he should have answered. What he should have said back was "Madame, why aren't you?"

That, in fact, is just the kind of question that needs to be asked of feminists these days: How about you? The principle is simple and universal, grasped instinctively by children and elaborated throughout the most Byzantine codes of justice: even-steven. Sauce for the gander; sauce for the goose.

I saw a glimmer of it breaking through during the trial scene in *Kramer vs. Kramer:* "By the same token," begins Dustin Hoffman, as I recall, and goes on to suggest that the same liberated principles that allow his wife to walk out on him at will might permit him to keep the child.

THE **MYTH** OF THE **MONSTROUS MALE**

(In real life, of course, Meryl Streep would never have given the kid back in the last scene; she would have taken him off to California, whence she would have extracted enough alimony and child support to run her husband raggeder than ever and make Jane Alexander change her mind completely about how much more human and caring Dustin was becoming; at some point both women would probably have met over quiche and talked about what a money-grubber that man was.)

"By the same token . . ." Exactly, Dustin, only get that quaver out of your voice—it's your *rights* that you're talking about.

Midway between the trivial and the grand lies that friendly-to-intimate realm where men and women meet and work out their lives in relation to one another: to wit, sex, often sublimated or displaced in curious ways. The issue here is geometric in the clarity of its resolution: (1) Should men strive to become more the way women used to try to be (chaste), or (2) should women strive to be the way men used to be (not chaste at all, if they could help it), or (3) should there be some common middle ground agreed on? This, I predict, is going to become *the* central issue of the feminist controversy; it is certainly the issue over which there is the most confusion at the moment.

There was a time not long ago when that issue seemed settled once and for all: Women had settled it, by opting to make it much less of an issue than it had been before. There's no question that by and large that is still the case, and that the results have been profound and almost all to the good: As Neil and I both remember, men and women today understand and respect one another to a degree that once seemed unimaginable, and in general get along much better than before.

But Neil sees signs that things are on the verge of changing back, and he is not making them up. I myself

242

have noticed among the students I see a return—with what degree of irony I cannot say—to such Fifties shibboleths as "slut" and "reputation," and evidence that the interchange of sexual values has not gone as deep as we may think.

In 1980, Professor Russell Vanoy could report in *Sex Without Love:*

> The traditional claim that females feel themselves degraded by loveless sex is certainly confirmed by surveys in my own undergraduate class, "Philosophies of Love and Sex," taught to more than two thousand students over the past ten years. Nearly 80 percent of the young women in my surveys clearly preferred sex with someone who loved them. The young men, on the other hand, registered quite the opposite view; slightly less than 20 percent found deep emotional involvement to be of any significant importance.

Similar surveys in my own "Battle Between the Sexes" course have produced similar results. "All empirical evidence," writes William O'Rourke in his 1981 sexual memoir *Idle Hands,* "keeps affirming the fact that women consent: perhaps it is changed for the young going through puberty now, but I was always in a state of wanting and women were in the position of denying." The old story, in short.

In any event, nothing is so clear about the drift of feminism today as the extraordinary extent to which it is activated by a desire to return us to that old story—men supplicating, women yielding or not yielding. Midge Decter observed it ten years ago, and it is much truer now: These women want that power back, whatever the cost to themselves. The seemingly settled issue of which sex is going to adopt the other's sexual ethos is, if these women have anything to say about it, coming back for renegotiation.

THE **MYTH** OF THE **MONSTROUS MALE**

History, conveniently, has supplied examples of both ways in which the negotiation can take place. One example comes from the first coordinated feminist movement recorded: the revolt in 215 B.C. of the Roman women against the Oppian Law and their subsequent winning of more and more rights from the state. The condition of that liberation seems to have been that they behave as much like men as possible, with all the traditional male liberty and callousness, especially when it came to sex. Hence: Messalina and Poppaea; orgies; Petronius and Juvenal tearing their hair about the unnatural forwardness of the new woman; even, some have said, the famous, never-to-be-forgotten decline and fall of the Roman Empire. It can be urged (Amaury de Riencourt has argued it cogently, in his book *Sex and Power in History*) that the rise of the ascetic creed of Christianity, which, despite all the feminist bad press given to Saint Paul, was and is a movement supported mainly by women, was to a considerable extent due to the Roman women's desire to reassert their traditional modesty—to be women again.

A second example, of course, occurred in the nineteenth and early twentieth centuries, when feminists tried to wipe out the double standard by bringing men "up" to their level. It didn't work, thank God.

A third possibility is what all my students say they want, and what for some time we have been urged to equate with enlightenment: the androgynous pastoral of sensitive men and independent women, where the women are about fifty percent looser and the men about fifty percent choosier than they were before.

That sounds fine—who can be against independence and sensitivity? And what American can object to a compromise? But aside from the dubious desirability of a campaign to make us, in this airport age, even more like one another than we already are, there remains the stubborn fact that certain things can't be compromised, and that near the top of the list is the issue of whether two people are going to be lovers. "Sort of" or "I'll meet you halfway" are not satisfactory answers to the question "Will you sleep with me?"

"Will you sleep with me?" *The* question. There are, perhaps, two main kinds of "no" answers to it. The first is delivered to someone to whom one is not attracted; the second to someone to whom one is attracted. When it comes to the first, there is no essential conflict between the sexes; men, though under the traditional contract they have received this kind of refusal more often than they have delivered it, know well enough what it is to be not interested, and the dynamics of attraction and repulsion are not all that different for the sexes. (Men tend to be especially interested in looks, women in signs of money, a discrepancy that some women unaccountably consider to be evidence of their superior sensitivity and virtue; both are drawn, in Blake's words, to "the lineaments of gratified desire"—that is, everyone wants to be with a winner.)

It's the second kind of refusal that causes the trouble. A woman who refuses to sleep with a man she doesn't like is just behaving, as they say, naturally. A woman who refuses to sleep with someone she does like—someone with whom she hopes to keep up some kind of friendship —is asserting that, *as a woman,* she inhabits a separate, sacrosanct realm; that her womanhood has some precious, exotic value apart from what at less intense moments she may, God forgive her, call her "personhood." She is also, whatever she may intend or pretend, seeing to it that in the future she will be the one in charge when the two of them meet, that the man will be the supplicant. In other words, she is playing at sexual politics in its oldest form, and winning. Above all, she is demanding that he consider her to some extent by reference to an abstraction in which he does not share—that he think of her, that is, as an object.

And with that demand the balance shifts, dramatically and, in the long run, intolerably. According to the old order, the power given to women by their enforcement of the double standard counterbalanced, roughly, the power ceded to men in the world of affairs. With that second kind of power neutralized—with women competing equally in what used to be the man's world—the score shifts from M 1; F 1, to M 1/2, F 1 1/2: women in charge, still, in the private sphere; neither sex, particularly, in charge in the public sphere.

That, probably, is what most of the feminists with whom I have been disagreeing for the length of this book would envision as the ideal. (Some of them, of course, won't rest until the score is 0–2.) For some few women it is achievable—those sharp and pretty and young enough to get to the top using both their new rights in what used to be a man's area of competence and the old tricks from the woman's, alternating between being one of the boys and being the belle of the ball. (Perfume advertisements seem to have recently discovered the appeal of this type.) You can't blame them for using whatever resources they can in a rough world; but of course one consequence is that, for every woman successfully having it both ways, there is one who winds up with nothing—some Utica car dealer's middle-aged unemployable wife who comes home one afternoon to find a note from her husband informing her that he's decided to liberate himself and thinks she should, too. Ask her husband to justify his behavior and chances are his answer will include the expression "By the same token."

Because the fact is that whatever stresses it may have to weather from time to time, we do retain an idea of fairness, of balance, in our negotiations with one another. Further, it is in the interests of common decency to preserve that idea, if for no other reason than that protracted outrages against it predictably bring about kicking-the-cat backlashes against the weakest among us: The executive feeling resentful about the woman who hustled and screwed her way into the promotion he wanted takes it out on his secretary, who then informs her unemployed boyfriend that all of his sex are pigs and she wants him out of the apartment, and so on.

At the moment, the question of how the balance is to be maintained comes down to one of two choices: Women can migrate back to the home, reestablishing the old order; or they can complete the revolution that gathered force in the Sixties—they can complete the change in their sense of self that goes with being the provider as much as the provided for, the doer as much as the done to, bidder as much as auctioneer's lot, and in the process inevitably cease once and for all to think of sex as a transaction whereby they give something for something else in return.

Well, there it is. Who am I to be telling women what they can do? A man, and therefore someone who for the last several years has been the receiver of such public admonitions, from the other side. Fair's fair. Also, a man who, like Neil, remembers the way it used to be, and remembers that what came after was an improvement.

So here's my vote: Sex is nice; and the more of it, pretty much the better. Just because a statement is simple doesn't mean it's wrong. People who tell you that having too much sex cheapens it, that too much sex is like too much food or too much wine, or too much Brahms, that after a while it loses its flavor and makes you sick—these people are talking through their hats. Too much sex is like too much money, or too much fresh air, or too much knowledge. It is not, except by external manipulation, a finite quantity whose worth goes up and down on the commodities exchange of the psyche according to its fluctuating availability. There's plenty to go around, once the controls are lifted, and, at least for a time, no good reason left standing for holding back on principle. At least for a time: Most people will no doubt sooner or later pair off and set up house, as they have always done. Love and loneliness are powerful forces, too, and it seems safe to say that domesticity will always have its season. Earlier generations understood the desideratum: wild oats; then settling down. It's just that they forgot to include women in the plan. That remains for us.

Anyway, the choice is clear, although which alternative will ultimately be chosen is still up in the air. As I said at the beginning of this book, I very much hope that the changes of the last decade have led to realizations which will prove irreversible; that women, and men with them, will see those changes through to the logical conclusion; and that in a few years' time this book will therefore seem quaint rather than prophetic. But for the moment, that seems an open question at best.

All things being possible, the conservatives may well turn out to be right for once: Women, either because of iron laws of biology or an unsloughable impasto of conditioning, may well withdraw in disgust from the mackerel-crowded seas and flock to the first messiah who tells them suavely enough that they are special and ought to hie themselves from this grungy man's world. In which case our own age will at least have served to supply future generations with a focus for their frustrated prurience. Drooling schoolboys will read about how we spent all our time at Plato's Retreat, and wish secretly that there could be such another; historians will chastise us for weakening the moral fiber and failing to keep up the birthrate, thus allowing ourselves to be overwhelmed by Mexicans.

There are those of us now who know that all this will be nonsense, but we'll be dead then, and perhaps so will the idea of the new sexual order: Women will pucker shut like morning glories in the afternoon, go sour and cagey, and recede into their traditional redoubts; men will circle them like redskins riding around the covered wagons in an old western, and that will have been that. There are straws in the wind: Over in trend-setting Paris, the *Nouvelle Droit* is beginning to argue that sociobiology proves the doctrines of racial superiority; over here, feminists aplenty are arguing in their benighted way that anatomy is destiny after all (men are *made* rapists; that's what a penis is *for*), and beginning, albeit uncomfortably, to draw the logical reactionary conclusions.

If so, it will be intriguing, at least, to see which rationale of those available is dusted off to dress up what's really happening. Religious prohibitions? Despite the current vogue, I doubt it. Marxist dogma? Not here, not for long. "Natural law," as derived from observations of more primitive forms of life? Possibly, God help us. The alternatives all seem improbable, because they are all absurd. But *something* will be settled on, you bet, and men and women will find themselves like Czech pols at a Party congress, orating to one another, everybody publicly committed to values in which no one with any brains believes anymore, all the while studiously pretending to ignore the crushing fact of that great Moscow of the soul, the conviction that freedom is a dream. We will all become like those French of the Second Empire, as described by Marx in *The Eighteenth Brumaire of Louis Bonaparte,* when he observes that history repeats itself as farce:

At the very time when they seem to be engaged in revolutionizing themselves and things, when they seem to be creating something perfectly new—in such epochs of revolutionary crisis, they are eager to press the spirits of the past into their service, borrowing the names of the dead, reviving old war-

THE **MYTH** OF THE **MONSTROUS MALE**

cries, dressing up in traditional costumes, that they may make a braver pageant in the newly-staged scene of universal history. Thus did Luther masquerade as Paul of Tarsus; thus did the revolution of 1789–1814 drape itself successfully as the Roman Republic and the Roman Empire; and thus was it that the revolution of 1848 could find nothing better to do than to parody by turns 1789 and the revolutionary traditions of 1793–1795.

Thus would our daughters decide that our grandmothers were right along. That's what Neil thinks is happening, and he's often right.

Well, I hope not. It's pretty much up to the women. As usual.

Bibliography

Auden, W. H. *A Certain World: A Commonplace Book.* New York: Viking Press: New York, N.Y. 1970.

Barry, Kathleen. *Female Sexual Slavery.* Englewood Cliffs, N.J.: Prentice-Hall, 1979.

Bell, Susan Groag. *Women: From the Greeks to the French Revolution.* Stanford, Cal.: Stanford University Press, 1973.

Bengis, Ingrid. *Combat in the Erogenous Zone.* New York: Alfred A. Knopf, 1972.

Brendon, Piers. *Eminent Edwardians.* Boston: Houghton Mifflin, 1980.

Brownmiller, Susan. *Against Our Will.* New York: Simon & Schuster, 1975.

Chesler, Phyllis. *About Men.* New York: Simon & Schuster, 1978.

Connolly, Cyril. *The Unquiet Grave.* New York: Viking Press, 1945.

Daly, Mary. *Gyn/Ecology: The Metaethics of Radical Feminism.* Boston: Beacon Press, 1979.

Davis, Elizabeth Gould. *The First Sex.* New York: G. P. Putnam's Sons, 1971.

Decter, Midge. *The Liberated Woman and Other Americans.* New York: Coward, McCann & Geoghegan, 1971.

Decter, Midge. *The New Chastity and Other Arguments Against Women's Liberation.* New York: Coward, McCann & Geoghegan, 1972.

De Riencourt, Amaury. *Sex and Power in History.* New York: Dell Publishing Co., 1974.

Douglas, Ann. *The Feminization of American Culture.* New York: Alfred A. Knopf, 1977.

Dowling, Colette. *The Cinderella Complex: Women's Hidden Fear of Independence.* New York: Summit Books, 1981.

Dworkin, Andrea. *Pornography: Men Possessing Women.* New York: G. P. Putnam's Sons, 1981.

"Erotic Film Festival to Counter *Deep Throat.*" *Providence Journal Bulletin,* December 4, 1980.

Ellmann, Mary. *Thinking About Women.* New York: Harcourt Brace Jovanovich, 1968.

Fallaci, Oriana. *Interview with History.* Boston: Houghton Mifflin, 1977.

Filene, Peter Gabriel. *Him/Her/Self: Sex Roles in Modern America.* New York: Harcourt Brace Jovanovich, 1975.

Fleming, Anne Taylor. "Women and the Spoils of Success." *New York Times Magazine,* August 2, 1981, pp. 30–31.

French, Marilyn. *The Women's Room.* New York: Summit Books, 1977.

Friedan, Betty. *The Feminine Mystique.* New York: W. W. Norton, 1963.

Friedan, Betty. *It Changed My Life: Writings on the Women's Movement.* New York: Random House, 1976.

Gilder, George F., *Sexual Suicide.* New York: Times Books, 1973.

Greenway, John. "What Really Went on in Eden." *National Review,* October 22, 1971, pp. 1183–1185.

Greer, Germaine. *The Female Eunuch.* New York: McGraw-Hill Book Co., 1971.

Grimes, Alan P. *The Puritan Ethic and Woman Suffrage.* London: Oxford University Press, 1967.

Key, Wilson Bryan. *Subliminal Seduction.* New York: New American Library, 1974.

Krasner, Steven. "Mixed Review for Cover Girl." *Providence Journal Bulletin,* May 31, 1981, p. D 3.

Kristol, Irving. "The Feminist Attack on Smut." *The New Republic,* July 25, 1981, pp. 32–34.

Lasch, Christopher. *The Culture of Narcissism: American Life in an Age of Diminishing Expectations.* New York: W. W. Norton, 1978.

Lederer, Laura, ed. *Take Back the Night: Women on Pornography.* New York: William Morrow & Co., 1980.

Leon, Barbara. "The Male Supremacist Attack on Monogamy." In *Feminist Revolution* by the Redstockings. New York: Random House, 1978.

Bibliography

Lorenz, Tom. *Guys Like Us.* New York: Viking Press, 1980.

Mailer, Norman. *Miami and the Siege of Chicago.* New York: New American Library, 1971.

Mailer, Norman. *The Prisoner of Sex.* Boston: Little, Brown & Co., 1971.

Marx, Karl. *The Eighteenth Brumaire of Louis Bonaparte.* New York: International Pub. Co., 1963.

Millett, Kate. *Sexual Politics.* New York: Doubleday & Co., 1969.

Montagu, Ashley. *The Natural Superiority of Women.* New York: Macmillan Publishing Co., 1974.

Morgan, Elaine. *The Descent of Woman.* New York: Stein & Day, 1972.

Morgan, Robin. *Going Too Far: The Personal Chronicle of a Feminist.* New York: Random House, 1977.

Neff, Wanda. *Victorian Working Women.* New York: Columbia University Press, 1929.

Orwell, George. *A Collection of Essays.* New York: Doubleday & Co., 1954.

Palmer, Bruce. Letter to the editor. *Inquiry,* Vol. 21, July 7, 1980.

Pivar, David J. *Purity Crusade: Sexual Morality and Social Control, 1868–1900.* Westport, Conn.: Greenwood Press, 1973.

Plath, Sylvia, *Ariel.* Faber and Faber: London, 1965

Quinn, Susan. "Men and Pornography." *Glamour,* January 1981.

Rich, Adrienne, *Of Woman Born: Motherhood as Experience and Institution.* Norton: New York, N.Y., 1976

Robertson, Nan. "Marilyn French's Painful Trip to Liberation, Literary Success." *The New York Times,* November 4, 1977, p. 20.

Rothman, Sheila M. *Woman's Proper Place: A History of Changing Ideals and Practices, 1870 to the Present.* New York: Basic Books, 1978.

Rovere, Richard. *Senator Joe McCarthy.* New York: Harcourt, Brace, 1959.

Russ, Joanna, *The Female Man.* Bantam Books: U.S.A., 1978

Serrin, William. "Opponents of Flourishing Sex Industry Hindered by Its Open Public Acceptance." *The New York Times,* February 10, 1981, p. B 6.

Vannoy, Russell. *Sex Without Love: A Philosophical Exploration.* Buffalo, N.Y.: Prometheus Books, 1980.

Wakoski, Diane. *The Motorcycle Betrayal Poems.* New York: Simon & Schuster, 1971.

Wylie, Philip. *Generation of Vipers.* New York: Holt, Rinehart & Winston, 1955.

Yates, Gayle Graham. *What Women Want: The Ideologies of the Movement.* Cambridge, Mass.: Harvard University Press, 1975.